# How To...

# PLAY CONTEMPORARY STRINGS

## A Step-By-Step Approach for Violin, Viola & Cello

### By Julie Lyonn Lieberman

T0068336

To access video visit:
**www.halleonard.com/mylibrary**

**Enter Code**
**2734-3188-1183-7159**

ISBN 978-1-4950-4583-7

**HAL•LEONARD®**
CORPORATION

7777 W. BLUEMOUND RD. P.O. BOX 13819 MILWAUKEE, WI 53213

Copyright © 2016 by HAL LEONARD CORPORATION
International Copyright Secured   All Rights Reserved

In Australia Contact:
Hal Leonard Australia Pty. Ltd.
4 Lentara Court
Cheltenham, Victoria, 3192 Australia
Email: ausadmin@halleonard.com.au

No part of this publication may be reproduced in any form or by
any means without the prior written permission of the Publisher.

Visit Hal Leonard Online at
**www.halleonard.com**

How to Play Contemporary Strings
A Step-by-Step Approach for Violin, Viola & Cello

by Julie Lyonn Lieberman

Published by:
Hal Leonard Corporation

Illustrations:
Cellist Dreaming, String Tree and Extreme Pedal-board: Justin Meyer
The Band: Loren Moss Meyer

Cover Photo:
Leonard Cascia

Photo of Howard Armstrong:
Susan Ruel

Photo of Claude "Fiddler" Williams:
Julie Lyonn Lieberman, First American String Summit

Copyright © 2016 Hal Leonard Corporation
First Printing 2016
Printed in the United States of America

Library of Congress Cataloging in Publication Data
Lieberman, Julie Lyonn
How to Play Contemporary Strings
A Step-by-Step Approach for Violin, Viola & Cello

by Julie Lyonn Lieberman
Includes index
1. Bowed Strings 2. Violin 3. Viola 4. Cello
5. Music 6. Musicians 7. Creative Musicianship
8. Music Technology 9. Alternative Styles
10. Multi-Style 11. Looper 12. Stomp Box

# CONTENTS

# A NOTE TO MY READERS

I grew up in a musical family. My violin lessons and school orchestra rehearsals did not inspire me the way family sing-alongs, trips to Tanglewood, or folk music concerts and festivals did. At jam sessions within the folk music world, regardless of my technique—or lack thereof, when first starting out—I always felt transformed by the experience of sharing music with others in a creative setting. But at home or at lessons and orchestra rehearsals, my passion for music receded into a state of effort; playing the violin classical-style never encouraged a state of play. The required daily practice in front of my music stand did not whirl me way outside the material, verbal world the way jam sessions did. In fact, the two worlds were intensely separate: one predictable and ordinary; the other, passionate and inspirational.

I looked to my childhood mentors for the key to achieving a state of communion with music, but it was not forthcoming. This was confusing to me. Certainly, I understood there were exercises I needed to work on and improve. I was highly motivated, but none of my training was balanced with a creative exploration of music.

As far as I could tell, my teachers cared about my progress, but not about engaging me in the ocean of wonder and beauty that music can evoke. The magic was constantly boiled out through rote exercises and neither the conductor of our after-school orchestra nor my private teachers ever asked me what I liked. I felt invisible. It was assumed that they knew best and that whatever they doled out was good medicine or the correct "next step" in my musical education and should therefore be accepted as the standard fare. It wasn't even inferred that if I continued taking this good medicine for enough years, I might achieve an inspiring experience while playing.

My argument with music education for well over three decades has been rooted in the belief that every individual, no matter what age, has the right to enjoy music making at every stage of his or her development while building technique. After all, isn't the beauty of this process the truth that we'll always want to improve, to learn more, to grow? Isn't that because music has called upon each of us too intensely to ignore? It's far too easy to forget what it's all for when embroiled in the pursuit of perfect implementation.

This book is my contribution to your personal development and, if you're a teacher, that of your students. Yes, even before you can hold your bow correctly or play in tune, you—and your students—have the right to find and express your own unique voice on your instrument and to enjoy yourself throughout a lifetime of music.

# INTRODUCTION

### What Do We Mean by Contemporary Strings? Why Does It Matter?

Standard music education tends to look more to the past than to the future. This book will provide you with an opportunity to survey the skills you're missing and will supplement them so you can take advantage of all the 21st century has to offer. Let's journey together into exciting new musical experiences, exploring cutting-edge frontiers as we balance technique, tradition, and innovation. The exercises offered within this book have been tested with middle-school through college-age students and in thousands of workshops for school residencies throughout America and beyond. In addition, my clinics for string teachers at state and national American String Teacher and Music Educators conferences, as well as in my own summer program, Strings Without Boundaries, have enabled me to hone this material.

This book is the culmination of nearly four decades of exploration, research, and practice. During that time, I've continuously lobbied for an inclusive approach to string education: one that embraces the musical imagination of the world honoring creativity and tradition alike, while incorporating today's technological advances and respecting tradition.

### So, What Is a Contemporary String Player?

When you think of the word "contemporary," you may picture a wild-haired string player rockin' and rollin' on an amplified instrument, but I have a more comprehensive picture in mind. I think the string player of the 21st century is one who is in touch with his or her creativity and is not only adept at a number of styles, but has also brewed and finely stirred their own amalgam to play from an individualized voice—whether traditional, classical, innovative, or all three.

Even if individuality as a player is not of interest to you, today's musician, no matter what his or her age, can benefit personally and professionally by training for today's globally attuned world. This requires diversifying skills from those needed exclusively for the classic music of Western Europe or one traditional style and living in the place where all music convenes. Luckily, we don't have to venture far to find inspiration and knowledge. As the cultural diversity of our cities and towns increases, music from around the world spills from concert halls to living rooms and is readily available through digital technology.

Throughout this book and its online video and audio support materials, we will delve into right- and left-hand techniques, as well as cognitive and auditory skills needed to navigate comfortably across roots music from around the world, as well as popular styles and creativity. Our journey together will include "electric spice": amplification options and special effects, looping, backing tracks, as well as digital editing. And who knows? You may come full circle only to return to your original style of preference, but undoubtedly with a deeper understanding—and hopefully with greater resources to use to enrich your playing.

### A Note About the Structure of This Book

Feel at liberty to zigzag through the practice exercises in this book in the manner most useful to you. Each unit provides a new set of skills without being dependent on any other, allowing you to explore freely as it suits your needs.

## Contemporary Strings Touchstones

- Creative Musicianship

- Multi-cultural Bowings and Left-Hand Techniques

- Multi-cultural Rhythmic Grooves

- Leadership

- Creative Conducting

- Technology as a Tool for Performance, Composition, Arranging, and Improvisation

## The Myths

Traditional roots players tend to think that classical technique is only for classical players, while classically trained string players tend to think they would have to degrade their technique to play traditional styles. Neither is true.

Further, almost every teacher believes his or her system is the only right way. That's not true, either. There are just as many ways to hold the bow as there are ways to hold one's instrument, regardless of style. And every style of music on this planet offers technical and musical challenges we can benefit from.

With that in mind, let's embrace it all and use whatever will serve your personal vision for what you wish to experience and create on your instrument.

## Pitfalls for the Classically Trained

If your background includes classical studies, chances are good that you've worked hard to develop an even, rolling vibrato. You've probably spent time working on scales, etudes, and pieces of music that tend to place the emphasis on the first beat of each measure, the downbeat. You may have mastered the dynamics assigned to passages. But the sum total of the habits you've instilled into both hands will tend to produce an even-tempered pressure into the string when attempting to play other styles. I call this phenomenon the "Vibrato Legato Syndrome." It's a habit you may not even hear or feel, but it will iron out the differences between styles such that you'll make every genre sound like it was invented in Western Europe. This book will provide you with the most potent approaches to widening your sonic vocabulary on your instrument.

Learning to vary pressure into the string, vary types of vibrato or leave it out, will help lead the way into capturing the unique rhythmic feel other styles offer. I like to think of "the groove" as the river that lies beneath the melody, the rhythmic subtext upon which all the notes ride.

## Pitfalls for Traditional Roots Players

If you are self-taught and have learned tunes by ear, there are a few traits you might have in common with other players from the same background: You may not know the names of the notes you are playing, the key you're playing in, or anything about the chords that act as the scaffolding for each tune.

If this is the case, some of the theory-oriented language in this book may slow you down at first. But if you take it a step at a time, you will learn your repertoire on a deeper level and increase your ability to do far more interesting things with the tunes you play.

# Why Change?

"Why change my technique or learn anything outside my preferred style?" Many players engaged in Appalachian, Irish, and other roots styles have asked me this question in private lessons. Conversely, classically trained string teachers I've had contact with over the years have either embraced the idea of widening their exposure or have dismissed it without even investigating what they might be missing out on.

My answer is this: "Obviously, you don't have to." But, as stated earlier, exploring new areas of musicianship will give you access to more possibilities on your instrument.

Your training background may have prepared you for familiarity with certain keys above others, and those keys may have fallen into three categories: major, minor, or Mixolydian (a major scale with a flatted seventh). Playing the music of the world will call on you to expand this vocabulary. You will be strengthening the "muscle" in your brain that's in charge of maps, of spatial relationships, to master new tonal settings and their unique configuration of pitches more quickly and thoroughly. You will find useful exercises throughout this book in that regard.

## Should I Practice or Teach Differently?

New skills require new practice techniques. I recommend that you rotate through six elements for the content of your practice sessions or class rehearsals, weaving between them as time allows. A new and comprehensive skill set will become available incrementally over time, built layer by layer.

### 1) Technique: left- and right-hand

Each style requires specific left- and right-hand techniques. Devote a little time to isolate new bow-strokes and new left-hand material within each practice session.

### 2) Aural- vs. Visual-based Skills

If you are accustomed to mastering new pieces by reading them from sheet music, try at least to supplement your learning process by listening to recorded examples of each new tune or piece of music. The visual "muscle" in the brain is already quite strong. Music is obviously an ear-based activity; so, the more you can feed your ears, the better.

### 3) Creative Musicianship

There are few styles of music worldwide that don't include a form of improvisation. Even classical music offers the cadenza as the vehicle for each artist's own voice to shine through.

If you require a piece of paper to summon a single note on your instrument, or if you always turn to memory to play, you will now have an opportunity to explore your own ideas.

After all, when you first learned to speak, I doubt it would have been acceptable to be told from that day forward you would be allowed to speak only when reading from a script. Right? Why should that be acceptable to you when it comes to the art of creating music?

### 4) Genre-Based Skills (Groove, Ornamentation)

Learning to speak words from another language without shaping the tongue and lips differently does not amount to speaking that language. Learning to play in a new style will require the ability to listen for and pattern your notes according to the phrasing of that genre.

Each style you work on will require a different rhythmic feel, style-specific ornamentation, and an understanding of its unique characteristics. There are a number of specific practice techniques you can apply to develop these skills.

### 5) Repertoire

Every genre includes its own body of repertoire. This does not mean its practitioners must know every single piece in that repertoire. For instance, five Irish fiddlers may play roughly a thousand fiddle tunes each and know only a handful in common with one another.

Listen to tunes in the style that interests you and then choose the melodies you love the most.

### 6) Technology

Whether you feel right at home or intimidated by cables, wires, stomp boxes, music apps, or music software programs, living in the 21st century will require navigation through the electric jungle to be prepared to play in situations where you'll need amplification, at the very least. However, you may discover information in the technology unit that opens up new opportunities you didn't know were attainable before.

To begin with, you'll need to familiarize yourself with the possibilities before choosing how and where you want to invest your time and money.

# PRACTICE TECHNIQUES & EXERCISES

♫ **Listening Through "Contemporary Strings" Ears**

♫ **What Is the Trilateral Learning Process?**

♫ **Mini-Weaves**

♫ **Scales & Patterns are the Keys to the Kingdom**

♫ **Vertical Technique and Vibrato**

♫ **The 12-Key Challenge**

♫ **Capturing the Style**

# LISTENING THROUGH "CONTEMPORARY STRINGS" EARS

Ear training is normally defined as a process that focuses on pitch and interval recognition. It's also defined as a skill by which you learn to identify chords, rhythms, and other basic elements of music. But in order to travel between styles, improvise, and develop your own signature voice on your instrument, it's advisable to train your ears to recognize:

### 1) The style of entry into, fulfillment, and exit out of each note

Each style of music has developed an intricate, sometimes extremely subtle, signature note-to-note approach to the contour of the whole phrase and its elements within. If you listen to a slowed down recording of music from any genre, you will notice the distinctive way with which its players shape each note and phrase.

### 2) Ornamentation

The type of ornamentation applied to a piece of music can sometimes be one of the most important elements that helps define style. Learning to listen to details like the type of ornament(s) employed by a given style, where they're placed within the rhythmic phrase, and how diverse or frequently they're engaged, are important elements to take note of.

### 3) Inflection

There's more than one way to generate an accent, and, depending on the style, preferred locations within the measure or musical phrase to place that accent.

### 4) The mood or emotion the music evokes

Music has the power to transform our emotions and energetic state. One moment, you might feel like weeping, another, your heart is pounding, and then you feel dreamy. It's beneficial to study the elements in the music that motivate you to respond. Dynamics play a role, as does a fluctuating or driving tempo, the instrumentation, the key, and the preferred rhythms and harmonies. Some variables are difficult to put into words. They live just as much between and around the notes as inside of them. Train yourself to zero in on these elements so you can learn to incorporate more into your own musicianship.

## The "Thinking" Ear

Any one of us is capable of learning notes by ear without having a clue what key we're playing in, the names of the notes, or their relationships. And most players, when learning a melody by ear, listen sequentially, meaning one note at a time. "Next note? Got it. Next note? Here it is. Next note? Umm … found it!"

The same applies for playing and/or memorizing written music: You might tend to approach reading one note, phrase, or measure at a time and then proceed to play the music over and over again while looking at the sheet music until you have memorized the notes. If you tend to learn music by ear, maybe you've had the following experience: You forget a section and have to return to the beginning of the tune to get a running start, all the while hoping the musical choo-choo train will build enough momentum to reveal the notes you've forgotten.

In either case, nervousness prior to a lesson, audition, group session, or performance is justified, because the music has been learned using only a few of the mental resources available to us. So, before we get started on the hefty amount of available practice material in this book, let's take a quick look at the most beneficial learning centers available to you.

# Four Styles of Listening

There are at least four styles of listening available to us:

- Passive

- Active

- Analytical

- Layered

## Passive Listening

We have the ability to listen to music as a background activity. The mind will still track melody, rhythm, harmony, and even lyrics, but while we are primarily focused on a different activity. For instance, while driving a car, holding a conversation, cleaning, cooking, and yes—sadly—even while practicing… and performing.

While this is not an attractive listening state for the musician, we do have to juggle a number of mental and physical tasks. As long as you choose when and for how long this occurs, it can't possibly be detrimental. However, if you allow passive listening to take over your practice sessions, don't expect your mind to suddenly know how to focus on active listening during rehearsal or performance.

## Active Listening

Active listening entails audiating each note or phrase before playing it. When listening to other musicians, you would listen as if you are playing the same notes. Oddly, even without perfect pitch we can duplicate what we hear by following pitch-to-pitch relationships, rhythmic phrasing, and the physical act of playing.

## Analytical Listening

The recognition of intervals, harmonies, and compositional or improvisational choices while listening to pieces of music taps into an ear-to-mind relationship that doesn't come naturally. It is a trainable skill that may or may not come easily to you. The ability to recognize the internal working parts within each melody or arrangement can support faster and more comprehensive memorization as well as compositional, improvisational, and ensemble skills.

## Layered Listening

Have you ever tried listening to the news on the television while listening to a family member or friend's speak about something simultaneously? That's what I mean by layered listening. You are juggling more than one soundtrack at the same time and retaining what you hear. This is an important skill to cultivate for ensemble playing.

If you only listen primarily to yourself while jamming, rehearsing, or performing with other musicians while you press their input into the background, you'll miss out on a lot of opportunities to interact, co-create, and learn from everyone around you. Learning to listen to a number of layers of music simultaneously is particularly challenging for us string players, because we have to tune every pitch, but even intonation can improve when balancing our ears between solo and ensemble.

# WHAT IS THE TRILATERAL LEARNING PROCESS?

I encourage you to apply a slightly different practice model as we proceed, by focusing on applying three brain centers simultaneously to embed each exercise or piece of music. This is akin to constructing a hurricane-proof building. Since muscle memory (automatic playback) is the first to weaken and even vanish when nerves kick in, and auditory memory (hearing the melody in your inner ear) can be spotty if you're a paper-trained musician, this process will ensure a balanced learning process.

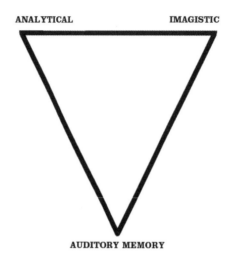

ANALYTICAL        IMAGISTIC

AUDITORY MEMORY

The brain has been engineered for economy of motion to conserve energy. For that reason, it isn't in its best interest to re-rig the patterns it has already sequenced. Therefore, it's important to practice trilateral learning for short periods of time in order to develop mental stamina gradually.

- **Analytical memory:** the ability to look at a musical passage and understand the scaffolding upon which it has been built, such as how the notes relate to the key, to the chords, and to the overall length and organization

- **Imagistic memory:** the ability to picture yourself practicing your instrument without moving your body. If you can get up out of a chair and walk across the room without moving a muscle, then you can use this part of the brain that is in charge of maps and spatial arrangements to practice this way.

- **Auditory memory:** the ability to hear the melody in the inner ear separate from bowing it on the instrument

**Note:** Muscle memory enables us to play the music automatically, often while thinking about something entirely different. Many musicians favor this approach to learning music—whether consciously or not—by practicing passages repetitiously. Our goal here is to push this learning method to fourth place in favor of strengthening analytical, imagistic, and auditory so that all four learning centers can work together cooperatively.

**Teachers:** You can include trilateral learning by including one small task per session. For instance, invite your students to sing or whistle a few measures of that day's piece of music while air-bowing the notes. Or, invite a student from each section to analyze one phrase aloud after using call and response to teach it to the entire orchestra.

If we approach new material by drawing upon these mental faculties in a balanced fashion, we can master the material more quickly and reduce potential tension about—and attention over—possible mistakes. We are then able to create more music out of the music. Let's get started.

**For Reading Musicians**

Choose a piece of music for practice. To illustrate the process, here is a phrase from the traditional fiddle tune "Tam Lin." This excerpt has been transposed down a fifth to accommodate viola and cello.

**1) Analytical brain practice:** Before playing the phrase, analyze the notes in relationship to the key. It would be more typical for most players to repeat a phrase again and again to lock it in, but if you take the time to notice its contours, you'll be able to memorize it before you've even heard or played it.

For instance, at first glance, it looks like we're in the key of F. But if we are looking at the melody notes of the tune, we see and hear the fact that they continually revolve around and resolve to a D, so we're actually in D minor. If you don't know how to grab this information by eye, you can play the tune and sing or whistle the core tone your ears constantly guide you to.

Next, compare the pitches to the notes of the D Dorian scale (♭3 and ♭7) and its arpeggio:

You will notice that the melody moves from the octave down the interval of a 4th from a D to an A. The A is the 5th of the key. How would you know that? Your instrument is tuned in 5ths, so picture the open D string and picture the next string up, the A string.

Then, the melody moves from the ♭3rd of the key (because we're in D minor) to the 5th. The third and fourth measures are an exact mirror of the first two measures, except down a whole step in pitch. You could also think of the mirror in those second two measures as taking place in the key of C major (same scale tones as D minor).

Okay, did your brain go to sleep? Did you skim through my analysis and figure that you'll wrestle with music theory later on? Here's a suggestion: Try to familiarize yourself with one small element at a time. Start with finding the 5th of each key you tend to play in most.

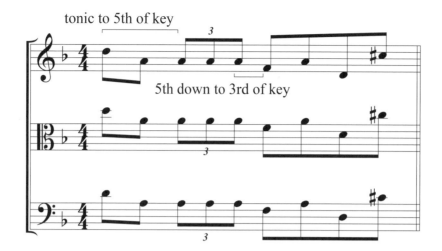

tonic to 5th of key

5th down to 3rd of key

**2) Imagistic brain practice:** Try visualizing each note of the melody before drawing your bow. If this is new to you, start out by picturing yourself playing your open D and A strings with your bow, or visualize playing the D minor scale with one bow per note. Eventually, you'll be able to play complex pieces of music mentally without squirming.

**3) Auditory brain practice:** Sing or whistle the melodic phrase or entire piece.

### For Musicians Who Learn by Ear

If you learn all your material by ear, here are some practice steps you can apply to build up this trilateral approach to learning:

- Learn the phrase of tune by ear.

- Visualize playing the notes on your instrument without moving your left hand while naming the notes and/or fingerings.

- Practice audiating and visualizing the notes a millisecond before fingering them.

**Analytical Brain:** Speak the note names or relationships out loud, using whatever knowledge you already have. That might translate into something like, "Octave note drops to open string, bow open string three times quickly, then zigzag between high second finger on D string back to open A, open D back to open A," and so on. It's surprising how much this mental review can help lock the melody into place more quickly.

When noticing note and fingering relationships, any type of schematic will help. Here's a little guide for the key of D minor to help you get started:

Now you're ready to combine all these mental "muscles:"

- Sing the melody as you name and visualize the notes simultaneously.

- Sing the melody as you name the fingerings note-by-note and air-bow the phrases.

- Mime playing (without sound) as you talk aloud the note relationships: "I'm bowing the octave, then bowing the 5th of the key…"

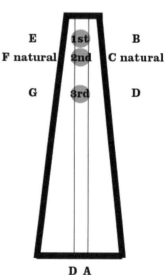

If you aren't accustomed to naming notes or identifying relationships, your brain will most likely tire easily and you may be tempted to give up. Don't. A few minutes each day—or less—will build tangible progress. I am the best example of this. My mind doesn't naturally process information this way. Over time, I was able to gradually develop this "muscle." Here are some of the benefits I've enjoyed:

- The ability to learn and remember melodies and harmonies more quickly and enduringly

- The ability to generate accompaniments to melodies

- Greater skill while improvising and composing

- A bird's-eye view of each piece of music I learn

If you're worried that analysis will interfere with musicianship, I assure you we aren't interested in turning you into an academician. We are seeking a balanced interplay between useful and important mental skills.

Congratulations! You've just taken your first steps toward mastering trilateral learning. Now you can practice with and without your instrument.

# MINI-WEAVES

Everywhere I travel, I'm told "I don't have enough time to learn (or teach) everything I'd like to." A mini-weave is a quick warm-up that enables you to introduce new skills while also preparing to work on scheduled repertoire. The warm-up may or may not have anything to do with the tune or piece, but the idea is to connect the two with at least one fine thread.

In classical pedagogy, we normally start with scales, arpeggios, and etudes for warm-up. In fiddling, the warm-up might consist of a new bowing pattern or listening to a recording of the tune we want to learn. The approach outlined here isn't tremendously different. It's just that the warm-ups are geared to accomplish more forward momentum from a different angle, the *Contemporary Strings* angle. The mini-weave can provide you with an opportunity to introduce a technique that pertains to a new genre of your choice, while simultaneously delivering an excellent warm-up for the scheduled piece of repertoire.

For instance:

- You can warm up in the same key as the piece of music, but focus the warm-up on a new left- or right-hand technique.

- You can extract a rhythm from the music and apply it to a scale warm-up for the piece.

- You can extract a bow-stroke from the music and apply it to a pattern warm-up.

- You can spotlight a chord sequence that pertains to the music and so on.

> A mini-weave is a short practice session that mixes a new left- or right-hand technique with a warm-up for scheduled repertoire. You can apply ideas you derive from repertoire to any key or any type of scale.

The following examples are in no preferred sequence. Choose whichever exercise feels useful to you and apply it to any piece of music.

## Mini-Weave Examples

Let's use J.S. Bach's *Concerto for Two Violins, Strings, and Continuo in D Minor, BWV 1043* (often referred to as the "Bach Double") as a reference piece. Let's look at a number of mini-weave warm-ups in the same key.

### Scale Warm-Up

Warming up in the key can provide an opportunity to introduce, in this case, the different types of minor scales we have. This might involve one new scale per practice session and could potentially sharpen how we perceive Bach's choice of notes for the Double concerto. Notice how I've included a minor scale from Eastern Europe.

> Why are there so many minor scales? Probably the same reason that one jazz melody, one flavor of ice cream, or one shoe design isn't enough to satisfy our eternal exploration of the human imagination, personal taste, and proclivity for diversity.

Dorian Minor: ♭3 and ♭7     Melodic Minor: ♭3 (and adds ♭6 and ♭7 when descending)

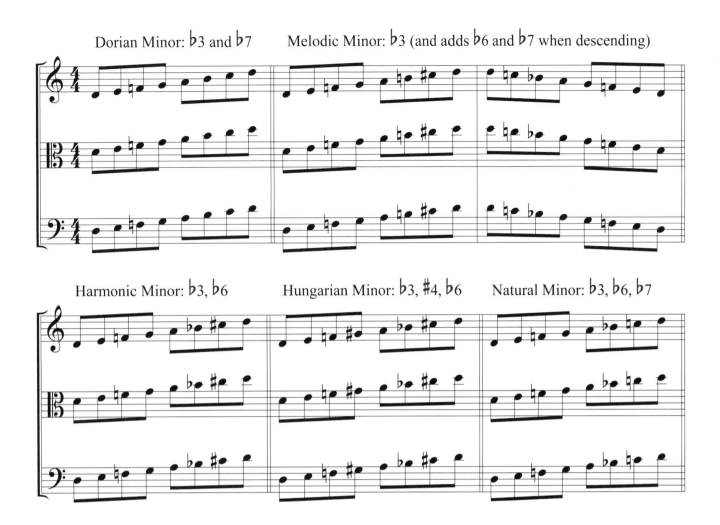

Harmonic Minor: ♭3, ♭6     Hungarian Minor: ♭3, ♯4, ♭6     Natural Minor: ♭3, ♭6, ♭7

**Mini-Weave Bow Warm-ups**

You can also choose a specific bowed pattern from the intended practice piece and apply it to the scale. For instance, in some editions, the Bach Double requires a hooked bow (two consecutive up-bows). This bowing could be applied to a scale or pattern warm-up before working on the piece:

Why not mix two goals together? Choose a bowed pattern from a style of music you'd like to master and add it to the warm-up for that day's piece of music. That's the beauty of the mini-weave approach.

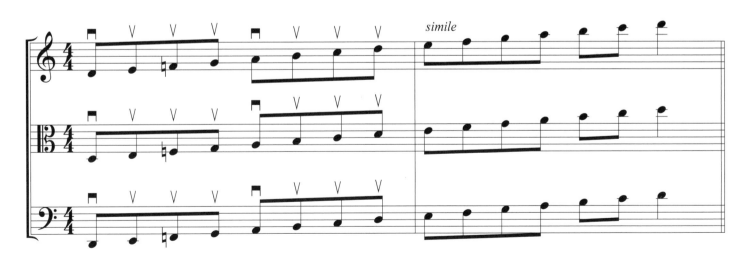

Let's look at another phrase from the Scottish-Irish tune "Tam Lin" in D minor.

Imagine you're about to rehearse the Bach Double, but also want to introduce a bowing from a fiddle tune. You can apply the string crossing from "Tam Lin" to open strings and then add in a left-hand pattern that uses the notes of the D minor scale:

Here's a shuffle stroke bow warm-up found in Appalachian, Cajun, and bluegrass fiddler styles. Let's mix this into our "Bach Double/Tam Lin" warm-up series. Why is the shuffle stroke important to learn? The emphasis is not on the downbeat, but instead, on the upbeat.

The shuffle stroke was one of the first new bow strokes invented on American soil by fiddlers in Appalachia. It's a long-short-short bow stroke we also find in bluegrass and Cajun fiddling, In the 1980s, there was a big push by rock bands to include Cajun-sounding fiddle into live shows and recordings. This bow stroke was a primary must-have for any fiddler wishing to get hired.

Along these same lines, you can introduce a swing bowing into this type of warm-up. This is a great opportunity to learn how to hear, feel, and bow with the feel you would need for early jazz, Western Swing, or Irish fiddling. Most bowed string players attempt to swing by dotting their rhythms. This is incorrect. Swing music relies on a triplet rhythmic subtext. Try warming up using triplets first:

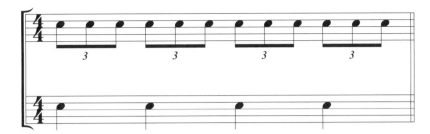

Then keep the sound and feel of the triplets in your ears as you practice the bow stroke.

This next bow-stroke can be used in a number of fiddle styles, as well as in swing and jazz. The bowing is challenging because the player must learn to draw a quick, light long bow on the downbow without a heavy accent, and then fit three notes in the upbow.

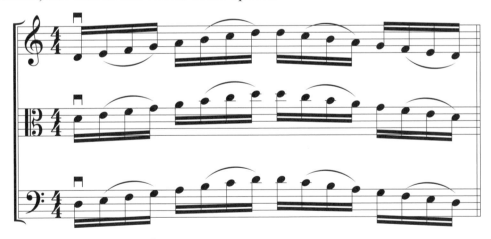

Now try extracting a rhythmic phrase from the repertoire you intend to rehearse and apply to each note of the scale. On the following page are three examples, the first from the Bach Double, the second from "Tam Lin." Notice how the third example adds faster left-hand motion to the same rhythmic excerpt.

The highly repetitive nature of this exercise, while maintaining an easy and predictable left-hand responsibility, enables both hands to lock into more challenging rhythmic phrases from the repertoire while warming up using an auditory rather than visual approach. Each time you stack the deck for the right hand, you are also deepening command over the tonal map for the left hand and the ears.

Now invent—or invite your students to invent—a bow pattern and apply it to the warm-up scale. Of greatest importance here, even more than what you or your students come up with, is the opportunity to learn to think on the instrument with independence. This style of participation on a regular basis invites ownership, whereas being spoon-fed by printed music invites subservience. And, this approach ensures that you or your students don't come to expect 100 percent of all playing activity to emanate from an external source. Congratulations! You're taking tangible steps toward becoming a *Contemporary Strings* player.

> If you are an orchestra director, you can cultivate student leadership by inviting a different student at the beginning of each rehearsal to lead a mini-weave. Ask that student to select a rhythmic phrase from his or her part, teach it to the group using call and response on an open string, and then instruct the group to apply that motif to each note of the scale.

## Mini-Weaves and Improvisation

Its particularly useful to introduce easy preparatory tasks for improvisation without using the "i" word. Let's apply the concept of the mini-weave to the basic variables an improviser works with: the manipulation of pitch and rhythm.

Picture a hand-woven rug. Its variously colored threads are so intricately intertwined that it appears impossible to determine where each color begins or ends. To locate the parts that make up its whole, we would probably need a pair of scissors to extricate the many strands of color that are joined together to create the total picture. So, too, is the case with a piece of music. We learn it as a whole cloth.

In this exercise, you can practice pulling the melodic notes out of a melodic phrase, and separate them from the rhythms assigned by the composer to practice manipulating pitch and rhythm to create a new melodic phrase. Here is an example using the opening to "Tam Lin."

Notice how I have pulled all the pitches out of the first two measures of the melody, and lined them up. Imagine doing this without using music notation to rely on visual skills. Your mapping system would be put to the test. You would have to visualize the melody as if fingering and bowing all the notes simultaneously.

Here are the same notes placed in a new sequence with the same quarter- and eighth note rhythms:

When you give this a try, continue to change both elements—the order of the notes and the rhythms—a number of times to generate as many variations as you can.

# SCALES & PATTERNS ARE THE KEYS TO THE KINGDOM

Why bother practicing scales? Each scale provides a roadmap to our ears, our fingers, and our right hemisphere, which is the "muscle" we use to visualize spatial arrangements and maps. Major, minor, and Mixolydian scales are not the only currency for navigating your fingerboard once you step out into contemporary and world music if you're classically trained or a fiddler.

You will need to familiarize yourself with pentatonic (five-note) scales and scales that aren't made up of only half and whole steps. But we'll get to that in a moment.

For now, let's start with the two keys that are the most essential maps to have in your toolbox: E (the guitarist's favorite key) and B♭ (the wind player's favorite key). These keys are to these instruments what C is to the piano, cello, and viola, and G and D are to the bowed string player.

First, make sure you are comfortable playing the scales and arpeggios using the most common roadmaps: major, Mixolydian, and minor. You will find these scales and arpeggios on the next page, but try to practice visualizing the map for each before playing.

Is it enough to run up and down the ladder? No. In a moment, we'll explore a number of patterns you can use to deepen your command over these or any keys you choose. Ultimately, you should also review Trilateral Learning and make sure you can image and sing each scale while naming the notes and fingerings. That's when you know you've achieved full ownership. Otherwise, you've temporarily visited the lending library.

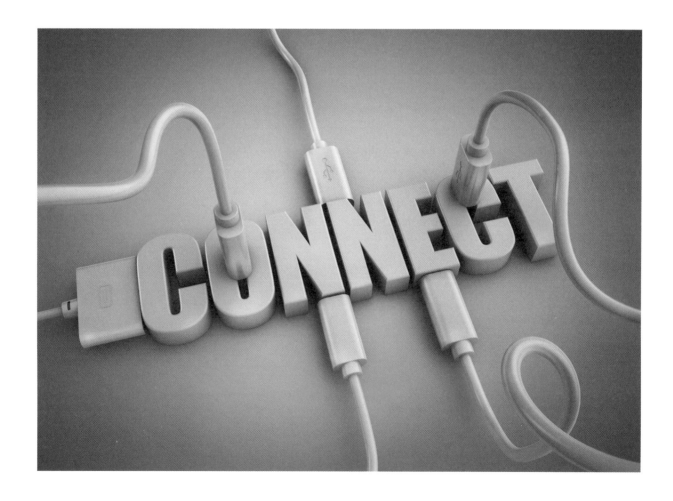

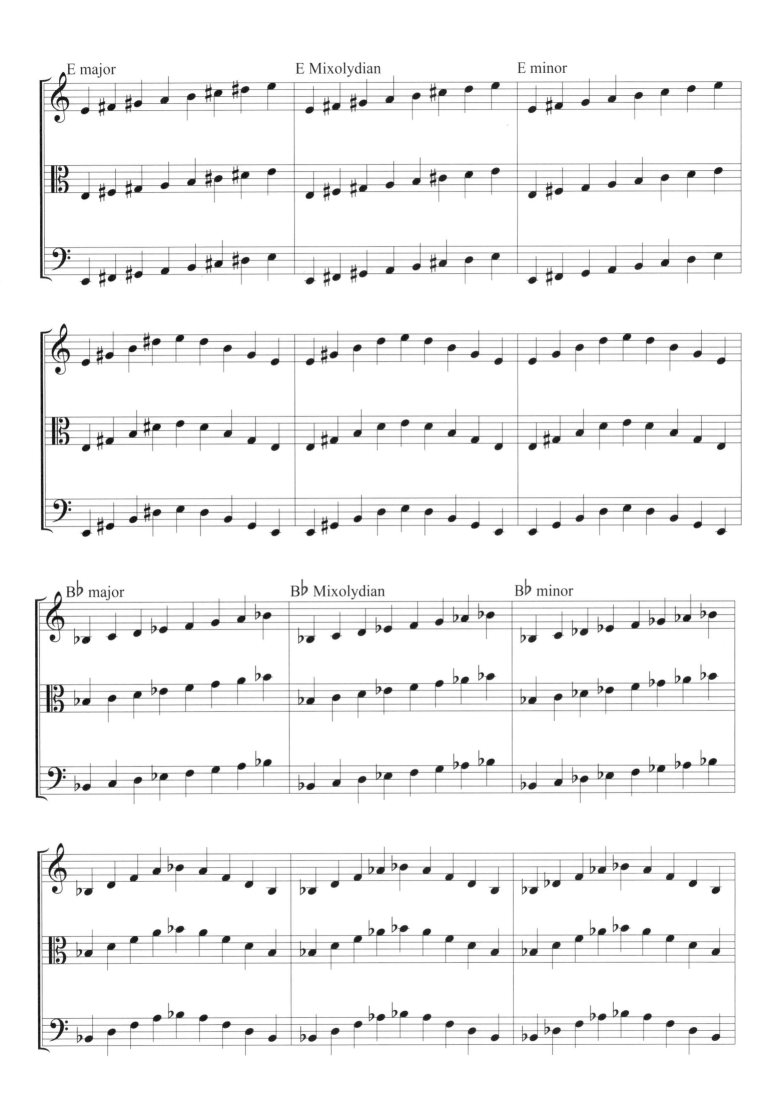

## Left-Hand Pattern Warm-Ups on Scales

Creative musicians often use patterns to master the notes they will need to have readily available when improvising. If the warm-up consists only of running the scale tonic to tonic (root note to octave), followed by the arpeggio tonic to tonic, this won't provide sufficient tools for fluid navigation across the instrument.

When we think of driving from one location to another in a car, we need to find a road to travel on, but there's always more than one road, and more than one method of transportation to get there. This type of warm-up allows you to practice picturing a tonal map across the entire instrument, so you can hop, skip, and jump anywhere at will with ease.

The first pattern is organized in groups of two in the key of E. This automatically requires you to jump up a minor 3rd to access the next group of two notes, and then the next. Study how each pattern is configured so you can more easily generate your own. I have provided you with a number of pattern warm-ups, but the idea is to make up your own or challenge your students to invent new patterns.

There are a number of ways to configure two-note patterns. Here's another possibility:

It's more useful to practice patterns across your four strings rather than tonic to octave and back. Explore every possibility in first position across before venturing into higher positions. Avoid mindless finger patterns that move up the string. The idea here is to catch on to the pattern and learn to apply it to whatever key and/or scale you choose by visualizing your fingerboard, rather than standing at the music stand, reading.

You can apply these patterns to any key you wish. We will use the D Dorian scale for our purposes here. Every Dorian scale shares its pitches with a major scale, found one whole step below the key. In this case, C can be found one whole step under D. So, you are learning two scales and keys simultaneously:

C major and D Dorian. This is a three-note pattern. Each bottom note is a scale tone, and I've stacked arpeggio notes above it.

Using the pattern you've just practiced as a model, change the note on top so that you move up a scale tone rather than a third.

You can combine arpeggiated motion with consecutive scale tones.

Any interval can be used to generate a pattern: fourths, fifths, on up to octaves and beyond.

**Perfect fourths**

**Perfect fifths**

**Sixths**

**Sevenths**

**Octaves**

You can also play any pattern upside down by starting on the upper partner followed by the scale tone.

Or alternate directions. I call this "Bottoms Up—Tops Down" or "Tops Down—Bottoms Up."

Let's try some scale-like patterns. Start on your lowest open string and run the notes of your chosen scale one octave up and down. Then start on the next note of the scale on that string and run up an octave and back down to that start note. Make sure you stay true to the notes of whichever key you've chosen. Keep going until you've played round-trip one-octave scales covering every note in first position. If you feel comfortable with shifting, then try applying this exercise on up through the positions. While you can make this easier by always starting the next round-trip scale with your first finger as you shift, you will still need to track the names of the notes to stay true to the scale tones and get the most out of the exercise.

Along these lines, you can play some games with scales to challenge your knowledge of the key. Try alternating directions as well.

It's said that if you perform the same workout every day at the gym—even if it's strenuous—it will cease to be useful to your muscles because they know what to expect. Let's think of your brain like a constellation of muscles and make sure to recalibrate warm-up material on a regular basis to continue to be challenging and therefore produce results.

As a next step, you can combine bowed rhythmic patterns with left-hand workouts in whichever key you wish to work on.

How else can you practice navigating the fingerboard? Sometimes, one small change can make all the difference. Now you—or your students—can invent new challenges.

## Pentatonic Scales

There are two five-note scales that will prepare you to play in a number of styles: blues, Gypsy Jazz, swing, and pop/rock. If you want to tour with a band, the singer's vocals take precedence, so you will need to be fluent in all 12 keys to be prepared for anything required of you. But for now, we're going to apply the following pentatonic formulas to E and B♭ to lock in the minor and major pentatonic roadmaps. Then you can apply patterns and trilateral learning to make each key your own.

Major Pentatonic: root, 2nd, major 3rd, 5th, 6th.

Minor Pentatonic: root, ♭3rd, 4th, 5th, ♭7th.

Notice how every major pentatonic has a minor pentatonic hidden inside it if you start on the 6th of the major pentatonic scale.

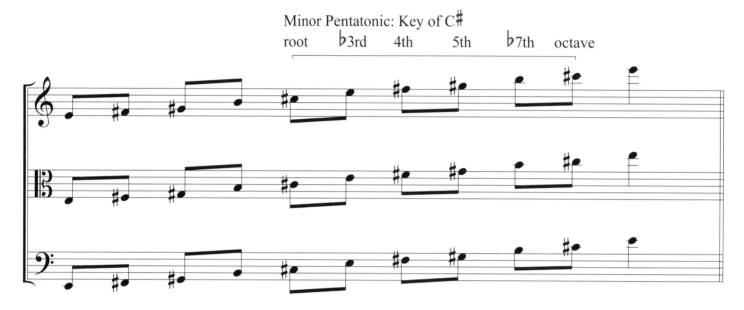

Now take a look at how every minor pentatonic has a major pentatonic hidden inside of it if you start on the minor 3rd of the minor pentatonic scale.

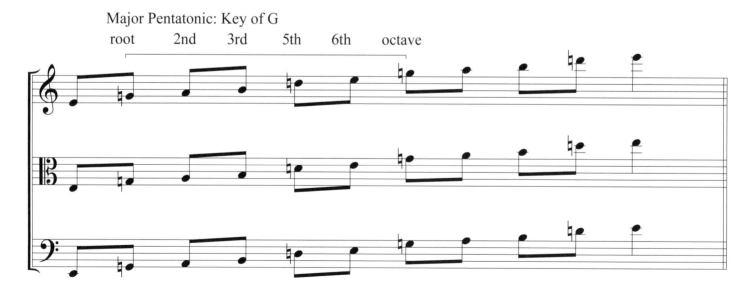

Scales that omit specific scale tones require the trilateral learning approach we worked on at the beginning of this chapter. This can take time, so be patient with yourself. Your auditory memory must lock in each pattern while your imagistic memory must learn to visualize avoid tones like hot coals and see each new map across your fingerboard.

Try applying the major and minor pentatonic formulas to other keys, if not all 12. You can also deepen facility with these notes through the use of some of the pattern warm-ups we've covered. For instance, here's the E minor pentatonic scale using the pattern of twos. You can apply this to one or two octaves:

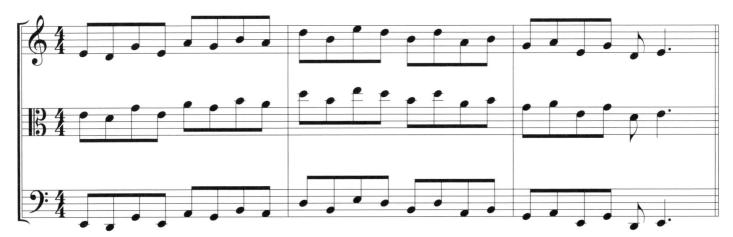

## Roadmaps to the World

Many other cultures sport a larger selection of tonal maps than Western music. For instance, South India uses a system of 72 scales (the 72 Melakarta scheme). The type of scale used can contribute a great deal to the identity of the style, but as we've discussed earlier, there are a number of other elements that combine with the tonal map to create each culture's signature sound.

However, if you're interested in deepening your knowledge of different types of scales, you can refer to my book, *Planet Musician*, for a glossary of scales from around the world.

For this section, I've selected one scale in particular, because of its inclusion of a gap of a minor 3rd. This can be tricky because of the stretch between the two fingers, making it difficult to play in tune. I advocate the use of the thumb hinge to make this easier. (See my DVDs *The Violin in Motion* or *Techniques for the Contemporary String Player* to learn more about the thumb hinge.)

This tonal map is only one example of many that include a gap of a minor 3rd and can be found in Klezmer, Romany (Gypsy), East Indian, or Arabic music.

Some Klezmer tunes will use the same map, but change the tonal center in the B or C section of the tune. If you think back to some of the scale patterns we've just covered, this is apparently a device discovered by more than one culture to create more motion out of the same seven notes.

## Chromatic Motion

To prepare yourself for jazz, it's useful to familiarize yourself with chromatic (half step) motion on your fingerboard. The fingerings you choose for this scale will serve as an important foundation. This is an opportunity for you to think ahead. What is most comfortable for your left hand? How might you use chromatic motion in the future?

If you aren't sure how to name some of the notes in the chromatic scale, start with the familiar and eventually master dual names. For instance, G♯ and A♭ are in the same spot on the fingerboard, as are A♯ and B♭, B and C♭, and so on. In some cases, it's just a matter of common sense: How you name the note will inform which finger you'll use. It's also handy to learn that spot on the fingerboard using both names and practicing substitute fingerings; that way, you're ready for all eventualities.

You can also apply patterns to the chromatic scale. Here is an example using perfect 4ths:

# Diminished and Augmented

There are two types of chords that can add a lot of spice to your solo. You can use their arpeggio notes or scales even when the chord changes don't include them in the tune: diminished or augmented. For instance, you could be playing over a G7 chord and suddenly launch into a quick diminished or augmented run and then tuck back into the actual chord and scale tones dictated by the chord symbol.

Diminished and augmented are more challenging to learn because of how their notes zig-zag across the fingerboard, yet easier because once you learn one key, you've learned either four or six keys respectively. What?! Okay, bear with me and you'll understand in a moment. Let's start with how to configure the notes correctly in one key.

## Diminished

The diminished chord tones are all equidistant minor 3rds. Notice how I've notated chord tones in the key of C twice. The first example is technically correct, but might be harder for you to play. In the second example, I've notated the pitches using *enharmonic* notes (same notes, different names) that play more easily.

The diminished chord tones are based on the following configuration: root-♭3-♭5-♭♭7. However, once you learn the key of C, you've learned the keys of E♭, G♭ (or F♯), and B♭♭ (or A). This is because each shares the same chord and scale tones.

The diminished scale is built as follows: whole step, half step, whole, half all the way up to the octave.

Learning the diminished scales and arpeggios can feel intimidating at first because of all the accidentals, so I suggest focusing on the intervalic (the whole and half-steps between the notes) relationships at first without even trying to name the notes.

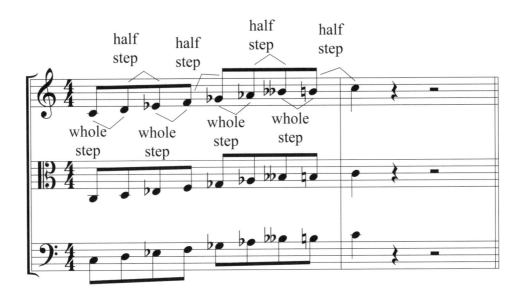

You can also benefit by practicing across small territories. For instance, in this example, notice how the root to minor 3rd is followed by playing the scale tone in between: ascending, then descending.

### Augmented

The augmented arpeggio is configured as follows: root-major 3rd-♯5-♭7

### Whole-tone scale

The scale consists of whole tones (whole steps). Notice how the distance between the augmented 5th to the ♭7th is the space of a whole step:

I highly recommend applying some of the patterns we've covered in this chapter to the diminished and augmented scales. You can also combine two types of patterns. For instance, here's a chromatic scale. Each note in the scale is partnered with a whole step from the augmented scale.

# VERTICAL TECHNIQUE AND VIBRATO

 **VERTICAL TECHNIQUE AND VIBRATO**

## Vertical Technique

I coined this phrase many years ago to provide string players with an awareness of an additional dimension to left-hand technique that can:

- Promote greater facility and therefore speed

- Provide the ability to create a range of sounds required by styles from around the world: ghosting, Arabic and East Indian slide techniques, slide technique in general, and the *vibraslide*

To master as specific a control over finger pressure as you've strived to gain over intonation (tuned pitch), picture a container of space that can be subdivided into 100 units. This model can be—and has been by ethnomusicologists—applied to pitch, and is called "100 cents." The cent is a logarithmic unit of measure used for musical intervals, so 100 cents equals a half step.

This same container can be pictured as the bar lines that define a measure and, depending on the time signature, that container will hold as few or as many units of time as the composer intends.

So now, turn this container on its side. Its bottom line defines the fingerboard and its top line defines your strings, when at rest. One-hundred percent pressure describes the fingertip when pressing the string down to touch the fingerboard. Zero-percent pressure defines the string at rest, with the fingertip barely grazing the "hairs" of the string. No, your string doesn't actually have hairs growing out of it, but this is a useful metaphor.

Learn to master as many gradients between zero and 100 as you can. Don't worry about your bow; the gateway between the right and left motor cortices, the corpus callosum, will carry that information across to the right hand and it will mirror the activity. Eventually, your goal will be to gain independent control over the two sides, using gravity to sink the bow into the string rather than muscle power as you release left-hand finger pressure.

The vibraslide itself does not employ the rolling motion that normal vibrato requires. Your finger will ice-skate the distance of approximately a half-inch to a full inch—depending on the effect you wish to create—using about zero on up to 30 percent pressure. Varying width, pressure, and speed will enable you to produce a wide range of sounds. For practice:

- Start at zero percent: Ice-skate slow and wide; medium tempo and wide; then, fast and wide.

- Repeat this process using five percent, ten percent, incrementally up to 30 percent pressure.

The typical approach to vibrato for classically trained players tends to focus on practice techniques designed to master the width and speed of the roll. Once the player has mastered these elements, he or she is encouraged to apply vibrato to every note.

Unfortunately, the application of vibrato to every note when playing other genres is not appropriate. Some styles do not include vibrato, while others call for a more varied approach. For instance, just as slide technique in a style like the blues does not call for slides into every single note, nor is it appropriate to slide exactly the same way every time, vibrato is regarded as an individuated ornament. This can include:

- A tone colored by a bowed rhythm, texture, swell, or inflection rather than from the left hand

- A slower, wider vibrato

- A faster, wider vibrato that skims the surface

- A held tone that gradually blossoms into any number of combinations of width and speed, such as tight and narrow on through to ice-skating on the surface of the string in a fast, wide motion (originally referred to as "hysterical vibrato," though I call this a "vibraslide"); or any range in between, including fluctuations in finger pressure in and out of the string

If you do not know how vibrate, here is an exercise that will help you build facility as outlined above:

- Set your metronome to 60 bpm.

- Hover the tip of your first finger over a B note on your A string.

- Lower the string down to the fingerboard by sinking your finger weight into gravity.

- Roll slightly flat and back up to pitch in sync with the metronome.

- Maintain the roll as you transition from the quarter note motion into an eighth-note roll, then try rolling in time to triplets and then 16ths.

Repeat this exercise. This time, instead of rolling, slide the distance of a half inch while resting the fingertip on the surface of the string.

Certainly, when we start to work on any style of vibrato, issues with left-hand technique can crop up that might potentially block progress in this area. Examples include excessive tension in the left thumb, gripping the neck of the instrument between the wall of the index finger and the thumb, or any number of misconceptions re: how to generate the sound. But one of the biggest roadblocks often boils down to excessive finger pressure into the string. Let's look at how and why control over finger pressure is so pivotal to the skill set needed by the contemporary string player.

## Ghosting

Not every style around the world enunciates every single note the way classical music does. Learning to infer or ghost notes rather than produce symmetry takes practice. Here are a few steps you can take:

- Place your index finger on the D string. As you draw a long bow, bounce your finger down, then up, as if jumping on a trampoline. Try to use finger weight, rather than muscle. Apply this bouncing motion to a scale. Use a metronome and assign four bounces per note, making sure to use finger weight into gravity rather than muscular contraction.

- Choose a passage of music and practice gradually moving left-hand finger pressure from 100 percent down to zero and back as you play.

- Listen to string players in various styles and see if you can identify changes in finger pressure as they play.

Though I've already mentioned the corpus callosum earlier in this section, it's worth another visit in this context with the reminder the brain has a gate that moves information from one motor cortex to the other in a millisecond. This interhemispheric communication for the string player will naturally produce a lighter tone when the left hand relaxes and lightens pressure because the right hand will mirror that left-hand release.

When you first begin to practice variegating your left-hand pressure into the string, allow your bow to respond organically until you have achieved full control over finger pressure. Then, instead of activating muscle in the right arm to increase pressure, use arm weight down into gravity to help stimulate an independent bow arm. Experiment with different and opposing ratios of downward pressure and release between the two hands and track the sound variations you're able to generate as a result.

## THE 12-KEY CHALLENGE

Why bother learning to play in 12 keys? Here are six reasons:

1) All elements in music are made up of spatial relationships:

- The intervals (the distance between notes) that define pitch-to-pitch motion

- How a measure is divided rhythmically

- The inter-relationship between chords

And that's before we consider two or more instruments playing together. Moving an interval or melodic phrase key-to-key sharpens our ability to perceive spatial relationships between notes while hearing those relationships over and over again.

2) This skill is essential to playing blues or jazz. It's common to modulate a musical phrase through a handful of keys while improvising before tucking back into the mother key. There are also a handful of jazz standards that are performed in several different keys. For instance, I've come across "Sweet Georgia Brown" in the keys of A♭, G, and C. And, since players of wind instruments like saxophone, trumpet, and clarinet are more comfortable in the flat keys because of how their instruments are configured, it's important to build familiarity with the flat keys.

3) If you want to play in a band, the singer doesn't care if the key is difficult for the instrumentalists in the group. He or she will sing in whatever keys are vocally comfortable and it's "tough luck" for everyone else.

4) Playing in 12 keys challenges us to learn every single note on the fingerboard and it encourages us to work out the best fingering options, a system we will turn to again and again over the years as we learn new repertoire or improvise. In essence, we chase away any shadows lurking in our mind or left hand by shining the light onto every single note available to us across the fingerboard.

5) We can now pick and choose ornaments with clarity and control that will best support the melody or improvisation—no matter what style.

6) Moving a melodic idea with its style-specific ornamentation through the 12 keys will help you incorporate ideas from that genre into your ears and mind more solidly than playing one practice idea with the same notes as encountered in the melody.

So how do you get started? Using as your base the chromatic scale you practiced in this unit, try placing a partnered interval above each note of that chromatic scale. We've already practiced applying major 3rds above scale tones, so let's try a different interval, the perfect 4th.

There are two ways you can locate this interval from each chromatic scale tone:

- Find the major 3rd above each note and move up another half step

- Count out two whole steps plus one half step

You can have fun with playing in 12 keys by lifting a riff off a favorite recording, or taking a snippet of a melody from a piece you're working on, or even trying to move a song you're extremely familiar with—like "Twinkle, Twinkle Little Star" or "Happy Birthday"—through the 12 keys.

If you tackle a more complex riff like the one pictured below, I suggest you break it down into smaller units. This particular riff includes a ♭9 and a minor 6th moving to a major 6th.

For instance, you can first work on locating the 6th of each key by arpeggiating up and down to it. This is an intermediary step to visualizing the root note and the 6th simultaneously. Here are examples in the keys of C and D♭.

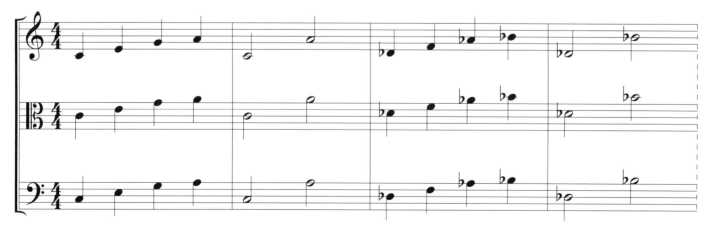

Then isolate the beginning of the phrase to work out fingerings. Make sure you can name each key and immediately be able to picture the ♭9 of that key moving to the minor 3rd and back again:

Now you're ready to practice the actual riff, moving chromatically through the 12 keys (ascending and descending) or using the Cycle of Fifths as demonstrated here.

# CAPTURING THE STYLE

There are four components crucial to your ability to sound authentic in any style you hope to master. Otherwise, you will sound classical on everything you attempt—or, if you come from a particular roots tradition, you will tend to sound like that genre.

The first step is to listen to the style you're interested in playing, take note of key elements from that style, and learn how to…

1) Convey the groove through how you move your bow hand

2) Include style-specific ornamentation, as discussed earlier

3) Duplicate articulation and phrasing

4) Learn the parameters of what is and isn't acceptable as it pertains to improvisation in the style that interests you

It's more effective to practice each of these elements separately to form new physical habits. That's because muscle memory is like a bar code: Our motor cortices record repetitive activities and lock those actions into self-contained units. This is useful: We don't have to figure out how to get out of bed each morning from scratch, nor do we first have to relearn how to hold the bow each time we take it out of the case. Conversely, these self-contained storage units, sometimes referred to as engrams, also make it difficult to generate new choices.

## Capturing the Groove

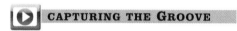 CAPTURING THE GROOVE

We have covered this topic elsewhere in the book, but there's always more to think about and practice. As already discussed, bowing with a driving, rhythmic groove is fundamental to roots traditions throughout the world, but conceiving of the bow arm as a "rhythm instrument" is a comparatively new approach for classically trained string players.

An understandable preoccupation with intonation and an emphasis on playing music through the eyes tends to produce a right-hand-serves-the-left relationship. In addition, classical training tends to foster a habitually symmetrical, downbeat-oriented muscular response coupled with a high percentage of either extremely staccato or extremely legato activity. Factor in the exclusion of focused, rhythmic practice performed by ear, and it's easy to understand why string players sometimes lack strong rhythmic skills.

### The Ears and Rhythm

Music is an aural art that has been visually organized primarily by one culture: Western European classical. This is understandably necessary to accommodate longer, more complex compositions, but I've found that visual learning can weaken the player's ability to hear, feel, and articulate rhythmic grooves. They sound more like facsimiles than foot-stomping, body-thumping, can't-help-but-dance rhythmic drives. Paging back through the history of music—before the art of performance—music was learned by ear, accompanied dance, and was integral to spiritual worship worldwide. When it comes to learning basic rhythms and rhythmic phrases, it's best to start with an ears-first practice plan.

### Practice Dedicated Only to the "Rhythmic Muscles" in the Brain

It is brain survival to maintain a system of economy of motion. Consequently, in your brain's world, it isn't beneficial to rewire every time you do something new. It will utilize old pathways. To develop the rhythmic center of the brain simultaneous to the left motor cortex (which is in charge of muscle moves on the right side of the body) requires new and constantly stepped-up challenges. Therefore, it's useful to isolate the bow arm during practice every day for at least three reasons:

1) The "rhythm muscles" are located in separate locations from the "pitch muscles" in the brain.

2) The left motor cortex controls the right arm, and should be thought of as a separate "muscle" from the right motor cortex.

3) Any use of the left hand dilutes attention and reduces or slows progress for the bow hand and the ears.

While practicing rhythms with the bow hand, it's best to do this by ear. If you need to refer to a written rhythmic phrase, play it once or twice while reading and then turn away from the music stand and repeat the phrase a few times on an open string. The visual cortex is immense (far larger than the auditory cortex) and science has proven that when the eyes are activated, the other senses can shut down as much as 75 percent. Therefore, to heighten rhythmic skills, it's useful to use call and response by means of a backing track: Tap, walk, bounce, clap, sing, or bow rhythms on an open string to feel and hear each like a heartbeat before playing them.

 **CAPTURING THE GROOVE: RHYTHMIC EAR TRAINING**

### The Bow and Rhythm

The same rhythmic phrase can sound unique each time you modify how you enter and exit notes, where you place inflection (accentuation) within the phrase, whether or not you cut certain notes short—including how you accomplish that—and the underlying "rhythmic subtext" you feel and hear while playing the phrase.

To practice each of these skills, choose a rhythmic phrase and play it, applying the following protocol:

- Use a legato, vibrato sound.

- Now remove all vibrato.

- Accent the first note, then repeat the phrase as you accent the second note, then the third, and so on.

- Practice abbreviating notes. I call notes that don't fulfill the written time value "clipped notes." Follow the same scheme as in the step above by repeating the phrase and moving the clipped note: Play the first note slightly shorter, then the second, etc. The challenge here is to avoid rushing the pulse, waiting the appropriate amount of time before playing the note that follows the clipped pitch.

**Rhythmic Subtext**

If you only practice or teach rhythmic phrases using a metronome, the cultural spice required to enliven and shape the identity of the music may get bleached out. Therefore, it's important to listen to the original style to ascertain how the band or ensemble moves and grooves behind the melody. This is what I mean by the "rhythmic subtext" of the style. For instance, when playing the fiddle music of Appalachia, if you don't hear and feel a constant shuffle stroke (long-short-short bow pattern with the inflection on the first of the two short bows), the melody won't sound authentic. Study audio examples of the style you're interested in and try bowing on an open string or on one fingered pitch along with the audio.

**Suggested Daily Practice**

Allot at least 15 minutes a day to practice rhythmic ideas.

- Practice quarter-note triplets and syncopated rhythms, because string players tend to be weaker with these rhythms.

 **QUARTER-NOTE TRIPLETS**

- Practice asymmetrical bow patterns. (See "Paradiddles" in the unit "Creative Musicianship.")

- Practice groove-related bow strokes by playing with recordings.

- Using a genre-specific backup track, be certain you can play the basic rhythms back-to-back, one measure each, by audiating first: half note, quarter, quarter-note triplet, eighths, triplets, 16ths, and so on. (See my DVD *Rhythmizing the Bow*.)

- Practice odd meter and alternating meter. (See my book *Planet Musician* with CD.)

## Ornamentation

Each style colors its notes with its own code of expressive textures and embellishments. The inception, follow-through, and closure of highlighted pitches within the musical phrase help shape each style. It's important to train your ears to identify this musical element—particularly since it's impossible to notate. For instance, you can subdivide a quarter note into three or four sub-units. Depending on the style, one of those sub-units may be slightly emphasized. That emphasis might be achieved through a quickening of the bow or an increase in pressure or both. Try practicing this both ways.

We're going to zoom in on what you'll need to know for slide technique since we've already discussed vibrato and a number of other ornaments earlier in the book.

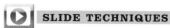 **SLIDE TECHNIQUES**

Did you know that each style has its own unique approach to slide technique? There are many variations for slides that are impossible to notate. For instance, in India, called *gamakas*, there are thousands. To master the art of the slide, you will need to integrate what you learned about finger pressure modulation in the unit titled "Vertical Technique and Vibrato" with at least three other variables: distance, speed, and bow pressure. Your bow hand will automatically mirror the manner with which you manipulate your left-hand fingers, unless you instruct it otherwise. You can add even more variations into your sound if you experiment in the following ways:

- Vary the width of the slide up into and down out of selected notes. First, allow your bow to mirror the motion.

- Try slow, medium, and fast motion up into or down out of selected notes. Allow your bow to mirror the motion and then oppose the left hand.

- Experiment with bow pressure across slow-, medium-, and fast-moving slides. For instance, you can start the slide with heavy pressure and lighten it as you move, or the opposite.

- Experiment with where you place a slide within your musical phrase. Avoid sliding into the first note of every phrase: It's the magnet all string players tumble into and tends to sound predictable and boring.

## Articulation and Phrasing

▶ **ARTICULATION AND PHRASING**

String players tend to listen almost exclusively to melody, because we've been trained that way. Learning how to focus your ears to catch subtle differences across each musical phrase will challenge you to turn your ears into magnifying glasses.

- Teach your ears to focus on the role of the percussionist, the bass player, or any other instruments that generate the rhythmic backup to the melody. That way, you can glean additional information you might not have noticed while focused on pitch-to-pitch motion.

- Choose a recording and listen for the subtle interplay between note lengths, the rise and fall of volume, and slices of silence across each phrase.

- Experiment with bow pressure in as many ways as possible. You can best accomplish this by subdividing one note into two halves, then three thirds, and so on as described earlier.

- Choose one note and play it at the tip of your bow loud to soft, soft to loud, as well as with subtle fluctuations in volume. Repeat this at your mid-bow, and then again at the frog.

- Focus on the portion of the exercise that highlights inflections covered in "Rhythmic Permutations" in the "Creative Musicianship" unit. Experiment with how you generate the moving accent. For instance, first, lean into your index finger each time you generate an accent. Then, imagine you're swimming the breast stroke and your palm is pressing through the water. This will enable you to create an entirely different sound to articulate your accents.

- Play the four notes with separate bows within one downbow, and then in a series of up-bows. Study the difference in sound.

# CREATIVE MUSICIANSHIP

# THE CHALLENGES

## Getting Started

What if I were to tell you that your muse would be willing to spoon-feed you an amazing journey on your instrument just as readily as the dots on a page or the tunes and melodies you've memorized? And, if you think you will set a host of white-wigged ghosts spinning in their ornate mausoleums, you're wrong. Composition requires that the composer live in a state of improvisation! Whether you're a player or a string teacher—or both—there are ways of engaging this learning process that eliminate fear, make it into a game, and create a fun environment within which to explore music.

Plain and simple, the brain needs to learn how to commandeer the bow and left-hand motion from the inner ear. This can be achieved while reading music as readily as without reading music. It is called audiation: hearing the music before sounding it out. When you think about it, why would you want to make music any other way?

This skill can most easily be developed through call and response, a safe, easy way to stimulate the correlation between hearing a note or musical phrase and finding it on your instrument. Don't have a partner, student, or group of students to practice this with? Record yourself and wait a few days so you forget what you played. You can use the same key or range through a number of keys. Record short ideas first (one note, two notes), then build up to longer phrases. Leave enough space after you play something while recording so the "future you" has enough time to echo it back. It's always useful and considerate to play the same idea a second time before moving on to a new one.

Call and response can be applied to the memorization of repertoire, learning solos by artists you admire, as well as improvised phrases. You can slow down a recording of a tune or solo and learn it by ear. There is even software that allows you to loop a section on a recording. Not sure which software to download? Just type the phrase, "software to slow down music" into your computer's browser or in the app store on your tablet.

Let's look at how you can push past some of the obstacles that may be preventing you from finding the freedom to discover and cultivate individuality on your instrument.

## New Perspectives on Common Thoughts and Questions

*I don't know what to play!*

Nor should you. If you did, you wouldn't be improvising. The brain is geared to turn to memory first. It's like an old mule that only knows how to move along one, overused path. You have to "talk" to your brain and coax all those little brain elves to focus on your ears as your guide, one note at a time.

Some tools are required to get the ball rolling.

You will have to figure out the key when playing by ear. If you're wondering how to do this without notated music in front of you, just meander around until you discover a note you like and then make the most of that note until you find another note, and another. The fog will gradually lift, and all of a sudden you'll have an entire key available to your ears, brain-map, and fingertips.

**Note:** This process is much harder when attempting to play over a jazz tune because many, if not most, of the tunes composed after the swing band era do not boil down to one scale. They also require ears for harmonic motion (chord changes) or training to navigate a *lead sheet* (a chart that provides the melody and the chords). See "Playing Over Chord Changes" later in this unit.

*I'm afraid I'll make a fool out of myself.*

All the more reason to practice the exercises in this chapter while alone, but you're assuming everyone around you knows something you don't. You're also assuming they're even listening to you in the same detailed way with which you are spotlighting your own efforts. Ask yourself this: Do I listen to every single note other players generate without a single thought in my head? Probably not. So why have you bestowed super-power listening skills on everyone else? They're probably worrying about what they're going to play, or what to have for dinner. If you make the most music you can out of a few notes, experienced improvisers—if there are any in that situation—will more likely assume this is a musical choice rather than an "I'm trying to find my way" default—unless, of course, you make faces while you're playing, or utter things like "oops" and "oh no." The secret is to make as much music as you can with the notes you have found.

And anyway, just because someone can throw a whole lot of notes around, it doesn't mean they're really good and you aren't. It takes a lot more than correct notes to make music.

*I need a solid set of skills before I improvise.*

Well, yes, that is useful. But the truth is, you don't need anything. Just your ears and your willingness to make sounds you don't like and then correct them. I boarded the "ouch… oh, this sounds better" train a long time ago and still go on that ride every single day.

*I just want to be right.*

There is no right or wrong when improvising, just notes you like and notes you don't like. If you're looking to duplicate the feeling you have when reading music or playing a tune you've learned by ear, give it up. Yes, it's a safe space to be in when told exactly what sounds to make on your instrument. But would you accept that scenario if, after you'd learned to speak, you'd been instructed to stay silent for the rest of your life unless reading from a script? I doubt it. So why is it acceptable to restrict yourself exclusively to other people's ideas about music in one of the most intimate relationships you have: the one with your instrument?

*I'm a teacher and I don't want my students to develop a horrible attitude toward me because I've pushed them too far out of their comfort zone. Plus, I don't enjoy teaching improvisation.*

Well, did you get a teaching license to win a popularity contest or to teach? Must you like everything you teach? Or are you committed to sharing everything you can with your students? Isn't it your accepted role to expose your students to new skills and experiences on their instruments? Let's not forget that, since 1994, the National Standards for Music Education has listed improvisation as one of the key skills we must teach our students.

*I'm a teacher and I have too many kids in the room. There isn't enough time to teach everything, and there certainly isn't enough time for everyone to solo.*

See "mini-weaves" in the "Practice Techniques" chapter for tangible ways to integrate contemporary string skills into everything else you are scheduled to teach without usurping precious time. And by the way, all your students can solo simultaneously. See the section in this chapter "The Looper as a Creative Tool."

*I'm an advanced player and my technique doesn't seem to help me. When I try to improvise, the accomplished sounds I'm accustomed to hearing from my instrument seem to vanish.*

Incessant downward pressure into the fingerboard in tandem with a bow pressed deep into the string is often the byproduct of a worried mind. Stop; lighten your pressure to 50 percent (see "Vertical Technique" in the "Practice Techniques" chapter) and begin again with a simple idea. Focus on enjoying the sounds you make rather than trying—*trying* is the key word here—to make sounds you will enjoy. Also keep in mind that it takes practice to hear a new idea on the spot and be able to articulate it instantaneously on your instrument. Allow yourself a degree of incoordination and your muscles will relax and be able to produce better results more quickly.

*I don't know how to play over chord changes.*

This is the bowed string player's biggest challenge, because we have little in our backgrounds to turn to for help the way band students do. In many cases, however, you can find one scale that sounds good over the chords. There might be a note here and there that begs to be temporarily (or permanently) flatted or sharped, so trust your ears and make adjustments as you go along. See "Playing Over Chord Changes" later in this unit.

*Nothing comes out the way I've intended.*

When you're practicing, try call and response between your voice and your instrument. Sing an idea, and then play it. Don't worry if you can't grab hold of everything you've sung. Just keep the freight train moving: sing, play, sing, play. Then play as if you're singing.

*I get off to a great start and then run out of ideas.*

This is common. Sometimes it's brain fatigue, much the way we'll utter some fillers while talking, like "um," or "uh," or "so." The brain resets itself at regular intervals. When this happens, don't push harder. Repeat an idea or lift your bow off the string, take a deep breath, and listen. Come back in when you're ready. There's no written rule that says, "When you're improvising, you *must* fill every beat with notes." Over time, you'll be able to build listening and self-coaching stamina.

Many musicians—when new to improvisation—think that when it's time to *improvise*, it means they should play constantly. Wind players can't get away with this because they need to breathe. Breathing is a skill worth pursuing for string players.

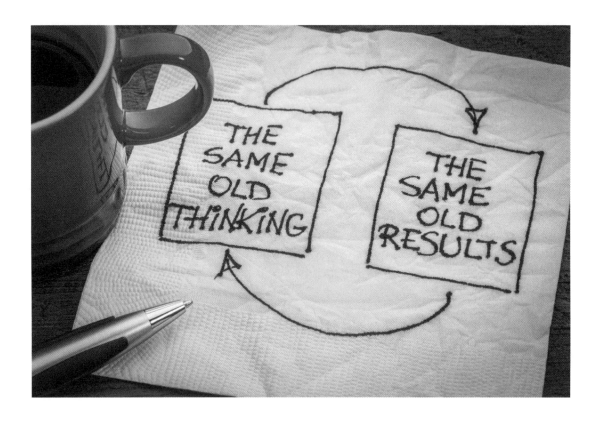

# THE BUILDING BLOCKS FOR CREATIVITY

If we boil it down to its essence, what are we really doing when we improvise? Mechanically speaking, we're choosing and manipulating a series of pitches and rhythms. Musically speaking, we're painting pictures: emotions, moods, energetic states, landscapes, kinesthetic experiences, dreams—and anything else available from the nonverbal world. Stylistically speaking, we're fitting all this into a groove, a meter, and (hopefully) using style-specific ornaments to help further shape our sound. And all the while, we're busy creating consonant musical phrases that have a beginning, middle, and an end (or a segue into the next idea).

Across this unit, we will explore how you can develop these fundamental skills. You will find that having these tools in your back pocket—along with a few other basics—will set you free. That's because, unlike what most non-improvisers tend to assume, freedom requires a support structure!

## Pitch Permutations

▶ **PERMUTATIONS: PITCH & RHYTHM**

Here's an exercise that will help you build up a toolbox of skills. It's designed to walk you through the steps you'll eventually take while improvising, but hopefully, by then, with more expression and playfulness.

Choose a key you wish to develop more agility improvising in, and choose the type of scale (major, minor, modal, ethnic). For demonstration, I'm going to keep it simple. I'm using the key of C major so we don't have to think about accidentals.

1) Play every possible permutation (combination) of the first two notes: There are only two.

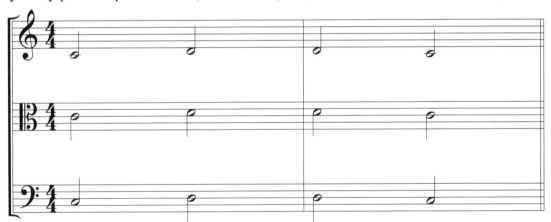

2) Play every possible combination of the first three notes: There are six. You can organize this any way you want in order to track the combinations you've already explored and avoid retracing your steps.

3) Play every possible permutation of the first four notes: There are 24 possible combinations.

In the example below, I'm starting with the lowest note and moving up to meet its partner notes in all the configurations I can find, then the second lowest, the third, and then the fourth:

If you continue to the first five, six, and then all seven notes, you'll find yourself well beyond 5,000 possible combinations. This could take days, if not weeks, so I recommend that once you've taken this exercise up to the first four notes, go back to step one and apply it to the last few notes in the second half of the scale during a different practice session.

Do you want to make this even more challenging and get more out of it? Go back to the beginning of this exercise, but this time, play the root note and sing each permutation from that note while naming the pitches and fingerings.

## Rhythmic Permutations

To integrate rhythmic ideas into the contours of your improvised melodic ideas, it's important to practice basic rhythmic skills. We've discussed some of those skills in the previous unit, so let's build on that by using the same concept we applied to pitch permutations. First, make sure you know your basic rhythms by practicing them against a metronome or backing track: half notes, quarter notes, quarter-note triplets, eighth notes, triplets, 16ths, and if you're feeling adventurous, groups of fives, sixes, and sevens. You can use my *Rhythmizing the Bow* DVD for assistance.

We are going to practice a series using eighth notes. This exercise will help your brain and ears subdivide each measure evenly and will assist your bow hand with timing and placement across each measure.

Set your metronome to 60 bpm. Play a stream of eighth-notes on an open string. Once you are certain you aren't coming in early or late, apply each of the following exercises with a good tone. Only look long enough to understand the system of organization I'm using and then play by ear. Don't move to the second, third, or fourth exercises until you've mastered the first one.

**Note**: It is beneficial to practice these vocally before attempting to bow them.

1) Move the accent forward every two measures.

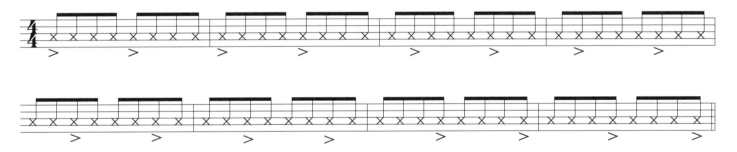

2) Now move the accent forward every two beats.

**Note:** You can also repeat steps 1 and 2 by moving backward: Apply the accent to the fourth eighth note for two measures, then the third eighth note, the second, and then the first. Repeat this procedure every two beats. Make sure you practice this exercise with a metronome to distribute your eighth notes evenly at all times. If you haven't already worked with the video clip "Permutations," referenced in the "Practice Techniques" unit, watch it before practicing this exercise.

3) Move the eighth rest forward every four beats.

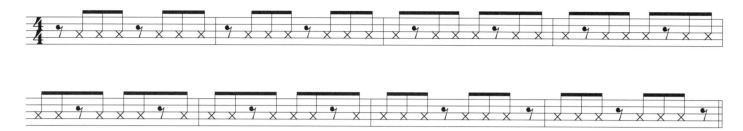

4) Move the eighth rest forward every two beats.

## How Do I Build a Consonant Musical Phrase While Soloing?

In every style that includes improvisation, you must learn to master the preferred time increment, the "container" within which the melody or solo sits. This, in turn, will support creating musical phrases with a beginning, middle, and end—though you will also, at times, opt to generate ideas that thread across to unite two or more phrases into one longer one.

Four- and eight-beat phrases are the musical currency of the Western world. Even in the blues, which is usually 12 bars long, or most jazz standards, which employ a 32-bar form, we find an underlying grouping of musical ideas that occupy four to eight bars. In jazz, the soloist often interacts with the band by trading solos with the rhythm section (bass, drums, keyboard, and guitar) over four-bar groupings. Popular in church music, fiddle tunes, and classical compositions alike, it's surprisingly difficult for beginner and even intermediate-level improvisers to create a consonant idea that fits into a phrase length they've heard and even played across many years in written or memorized music. We're going to begin our work with time increments using an even shorter phrase. But before we begin, let's consider the shortcomings that may crop up.

If you were to select any arbitrary group of 20 string players, regardless of style or level of proficiency, and provide each player with an accompaniment in an easy key, then rotate around the circle one by one with one single assignment… "improvise a solo for "x" number of beats in the key of ___," most likely, the same weaknesses will show up every time:

- An unrelenting downward pressure exerted through both hands that blocks rhythmic accuracy, often causing fits and starts outside the meter

- An inability to generate a cohesive musical idea across the required time increment

- If classically trained, a bow that tends to remain glued to the string in tandem with a left hand that vibrates evenly across every note

So, what to do?

1) Remove vibrato from every note. Vibrato should be regarded as an ornament that is later applied by choice in various ways, not fostered as a habit. (See the unit titled "Practice Techniques: Vertical Technique and Vibrato.")

2) Organize each practice session such that basic rhythmic skills are practiced sequentially until mastered. You can accomplish this by applying each basic rhythm across an entire chorus (the length

of the structure): a solo using only quarter notes, followed by quarter-note triplets, eighth notes, eighth-note triplets, and then 16ths. Then set yourself free. Here is an example for each rhythm over the same two chords.

You can use double, triple, or quadruple bow strokes per note if you aren't ready technically to move both hands on the faster rhythms.

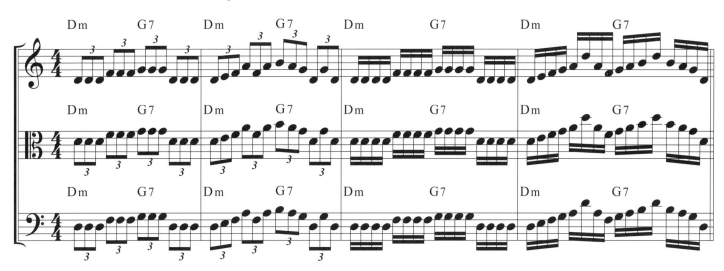

🔊 DM-G7 ACCOMPANIMENT

Practicing with this approach will enable you to develop the ability to play in a rhythmically accurate fashion while simultaneously inventing ideas. It calls for audiating and feeling each rhythm internally to place it on the instrument accurately. You are activating an entirely different brain skill than playing with rhythmic accuracy while reading music notation. Reading demands the ability to translate dots on a page via the nervous system into correct muscle moves which may—or may not—simultaneously include feeling and hearing those rhythms and the underlying pulse.

3) Practice applying slices of silence to each solo, even if in preplanned locations across each measure, to master the ability to generate new ideas while moving on and off the string. Refer to the section on "Rhythmic Permutations" earlier in this chapter.

Here are a few rhythmic patterns you might try applying across your entire solo one at a time. This is to avoid defaulting to old (or new) rhythmic habits; these are just tools to get started. The repetitive nature of a practice technique like this will help you lock a rhythmic bow motion into your right-hand technique before attempting to solo using a mixture of extemporaneous rhythmic ideas. It all comes back to the little problem we bowed string players have: We get busy with pitches and the right hand tends to go to sleep.

Try creating a few of your own rhythmic ideas to play repetitiously. Continue changing note choices

in your left hand while improvising against the Dm-G7 backing track.

4) Practice starting on the tonic (the root note of the key) and ending on the tonic. You can also practice starting on the 3rd of the key and ending on the root or the 3rd; or starting on the 5th of the key and ending on the root, 3rd or 5th. This kind of pre-defined structure won't be necessary in the future, but can serve as an effective tool for creating a progressive shape to the musical line.

5) Pretend you're having a conversation with a friend and try to "talk" to your friend each time you solo.

I've given you a lot to think about, so we're going to practice all this within a small container: four beats. I'm going to invite you to use a drum machine if you have one, or a metronome (start slow), particularly if you're teaching this exercise to students. You can also use the *Contemporary Strings* audio accompaniment. Play the riff as written. That's the accompaniment. Your challenge is to improvise during the rests and then come back in on time to play the riff on the downbeat of the next measure. This looks easy, doesn't it? It isn't. You may have to start excruciatingly slowly. Maybe even preplan what you're going to play at first to get accustomed to playing within this four-beat framework in the key of D.

If you start to feel as though you keep covering the same ground, you can try the following series of

**FOUR-BEAT RIFF**

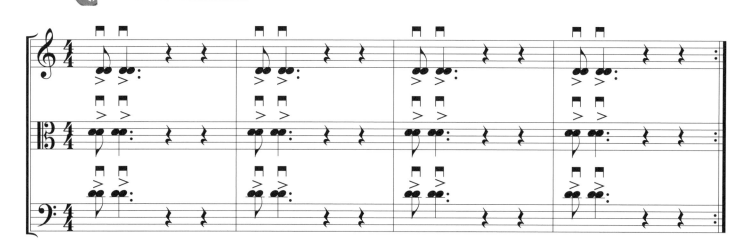

challenges to expand your soloing skills:

- Limit yourself so that you solo only on your lowest string for a few minutes, then move to the next string for a while, then the next, and finally your fourth string.

- Add elements we've discussed in earlier chapters: ornaments like slides, turns, and grace notes.

- Try to vary where you place slurs, how long or short you play your notes, and experiment with dynamics.

- Try using notes from different types of scales or restrict yourself to a group of notes you've chosen. The truth is, you don't need to use an "official" scale with a name. Make up your own.

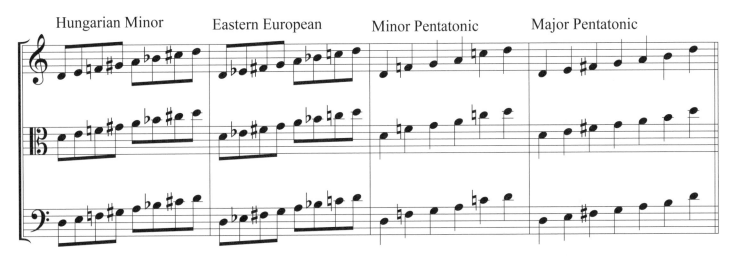

## Melodic Variations

▶ MELODIC VARIATIONS

Some roots styles, like Irish fiddling, approach improvisation by repeating the melody again and again, each time with changes in ornamentation or small variations that enhance the melody per the example of the traditional tune, "Mountain Road," outlined later in this unit in the section titled "How Can I Individualize My Sound?" To explore this further, let's play around for a moment with a few of the possible transits between two notes:

If you are trying to cultivate melodic variation within the parameters of a specific style, it's advisable to study and learn the embellishments that are particular to that style. You can accomplish this by listening to recordings and/or purchasing instructional books that focus exclusively on the genre of interest to you.

For instance, Klezmer fiddling uses slides, bends, semi-tone trills, and a grace note called a *krezch*. I have notated the following example a 5th below the normal key to accommodate viola and cello.

**Note:** The "B" signifies a bend. This is achieved by tilting the playing finger south toward the scroll (without sliding the fingertip) before returning to the original pitch. The "K" signifies the krezch. The grace note is derived from a scale tone that's a 5th above the open string. In this example, the krezch is applied to the fingered note on the A string. Since the scale uses an E♭, the grace note will be an E♭. The trill is achieved by resting the trilling finger on the fingernail of the finger that plays the B note; that finger is then rolled in a quasi-vibrato motion, enabling the piggybacked finger to "peck" at the string tight to the B note. (See my DVD *Techniques for the Contemporary String Player*.)

As you can see from this example, the melody constitutes only half of the activity in these two measures. The rest is ornamentation.

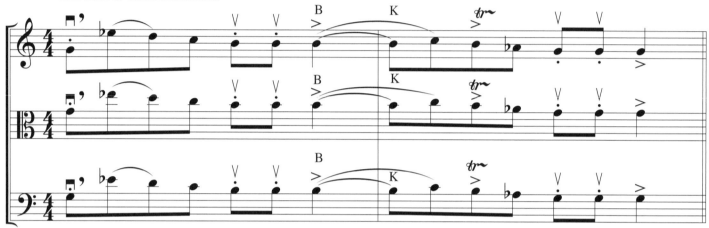

And, the next time through that sector of the melody, the ornamentation might be varied or there could be some new transits between, or variations on, melody notes.

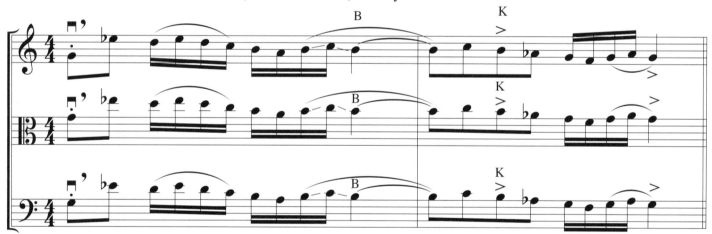

Maintaining the full melody in your ears is essential if you're interested in building variations on it. It's one thing to hear a melody apart from one's instrument, and quite another skill to hear it and simultaneously visualize which finger is playing each note in the melody.

The ability to visualize the notes as if you're playing them is the skill that would allow you to deviate from, and then return to, the melody. In order to build and test this capability, you can start to play a melody from memory (this exercise won't work if you're reading the melody off sheet music) and practice taking your bow off the string at random moments while you continue to hear and image playing the melody, and then come back in. If you need to place your left hand's fingers on the notes as if playing, and airbrush with your bow at first, that's a good intermediary step to take. The goal in this exercise is to hear the melody and imagine playing it each time you lift the bow off the string without actually miming, and then come back in wherever the melody has moved to as if you never stopped playing it.

Experiment with this on the opening melody of a tune like "Twinkle, Twinkle" first, then apply to a melody you're currently working on. Keep varying your in and out points to ensure you accomplish this smoothly everywhere in the piece. Try this, too: Pluck a start note, walk away from your instrument, sing a few phrases of the melody as you walk in a circle, return and pick up your instrument, and then start playing wherever your voice leaves off.

Here's yet another approach to developing variations on a melody. We're going to use a commonly played fiddle tag that most people have heard at one point or another:

- Play this tag until you have it memorized.

- Put on the accompaniment, *Contemporary Strings* "Fiddle Tag," and play the tag a number of times against the backing track.

 **FIDDLE TAG ACCOMPANIMENT**

- Practice starting on the high D and ending on the low D while experimenting with first clinging to the melody and then inching away from it—always making sure you can hear it, no matter what else you play.

**Note:** This is the epitome of the mini-weave we discussed in the unit "Practice Techniques." We could potentially embed just about everything discussed in this book into this one exercise: melodic variations, time increments, chord changes (the classic I-IV-V7-1), creative musicianship, and more.

> **String Teachers:** This game can be practiced alone, while taking turns with a partner or in small groups within a string class using the *Contemporary Strings* "Fiddle Tag" backing track. In this case, every other time through the sequence, everyone will play the "Fiddle Tag," and then each individual in the group will rotate playing the filler. This works well for two reasons: 1) The sheer amount of repetition makes it easier and easier to retain the melody and create variations on it. 2) In large groups, no one can hear one another solo so everyone can relax and explore without fear of judgment.

In summary, this exercise …

- Provides a safety net to return to

- Enables, via the sheer amount of repetition using a catchy phrase, the development of subtle variations across numerous repetitions

- Enables the player to lock into a popular time increment, the four-bar phrase, thereby making tangible progress in a short period of time

- Invites the development of theme and variation, of a progressive development. Many improvisers tend to jump from one idea to the next with no sense of transition between ideas. This practice system helps them develop threading techniques. "How many ways can I lead from the upper D down to the lower D within this time framework?"

You can borrow or create your own catchy four-bar phrase to apply this exercise to, or repeat this exercise in a different key.

## Compositional Variations on a Melody

You can also use notation to work on and find solutions regarding how to generate variations on a melody of your choosing. This approach will give you a tool through which your brain (or your student's brain) might be able to organize and move around pitch and rhythmic possibilities more easily.

Here is an example of the opening to a traditional Irish tune, "Mason's Apron," that I use as the basis for demonstrating four other styles in school residencies.

**Note:** This melody has been transposed down a 5th to accommodate viola and cello.

I figured that if I used traditional melodies from each of the five styles I wanted the students to hear, they might not learn as much as they would by hearing the same melody reshaped to fit each style. I was already familiar with the right- and left-hand techniques, ornamentation, repertoire, and underlying grooves for the other styles, so this made the process much easier. If you are planning to try to migrate an existing traditional melody into another style, it's advisable to learn a tune in that style, or at least listen to some recordings. Here are a few examples of the same melody over the same chord changes in three other styles:

**Mason's Apron: Appalachian Style**

**Mason's Apron: Bluegrass Style**

**Mason's Apron: Klezmer Style**

Here's how I approached rebuilding the original melody into other styles:

1) I figured out the chords that sounded best behind the original, Irish version. Then I generated backing tracks from the software program "Band in a Box" in each of my desired styles using that same chord progression.

2) I used a notation program to transcribe "Mason's Apron," and made a note of each chord over the appropriate measure to study the interrelationship between the melody notes and the chords. Then I set up the same number of empty measures as the original melody for each of the versions I intended to create.

3) I started with the Appalachian style. Using my Appalachian backing track—but slowed way down—I played the original Irish melody over and over again, gradually adding shuffle stroke and reconfiguring the timing of the melody notes so it all fit together smoothly. I repeated this process for each of the other styles and even rewrote the tune in a rock style with my electric violin and special effects.

Of course, you don't have to focus on style the way I did. You can just work on adding small variations to the actual melody in its original style. Experiment with the rhythms, the order of the melody notes, and the right- and left-hand techniques such that you hug the original melody, yet transform it. You can try this on your instrument, or play around with this approach using notation—or both.

> **Teachers:** You can hand out pencils with a worksheet that offers a phrase from a melody on top. Provide blank staff underneath for students to develop twists and turns around the melody.

# HOW DO I PLAY ACROSS CHORD PROGRESSIONS?

When a composer assigns chord changes (also called *harmonic changes*) to the score, this process isn't based on whim or chance. He or she is listening for the clusters of notes that will best complement and accompany the melody. These notes are strummed on the guitar or played on piano. The bass player designs appropriate bass lines by carefully selecting notes from each chord. The soloist, after playing the melody, will then utilize the notes in the chords to guide their pitch choices while soloing.

If you're new to working with chords, think of it this way: If you decided to lift weights for the first time in your life, you wouldn't be able to start with 100 pounds. Pretend there are muscles in your brain that need strengthening. We're going to start with one-pound weights, then two-pound weights and so on, until we've primed the appropriate brain muscles to function as needed.

## The I-IV-V Progression

A chord progression is a sequence of chords that follows a specific pattern, an interrelationship. Let's look at an extremely popular chord progression found in church music, fiddle tunes, blues, swing, jazz,

 **I-IV-V7-I CHORD PROGRESSION**

Latin, pop, and rock. It's called the one (I)-four (IV)-five (V7) progression. Did you wonder about the "7" next to the V? We'll discuss its meaning soon. Let's start with the basics first. (By the way, you've already worked with this progression earlier in this chapter for the "Fiddle Tag" exercise.)

Remember "Trilateral Learning" in the "Practice Techniques" chapter? If not, let's review this learning protocol: As you proceed through these exercises, it will be beneficial to visualize each note on your fingerboard a millisecond before physically playing it. Make sure you hear each note in your inner ear and name it before you bow it. We will apply the following exercises to the key of G.

Bow the root note. In this case it's a G. But once you walk through the steps listed here, I highly recommend practicing finding the root notes of the I-IV-V7 progression in other keys.

Now visualize the root note as if you were playing it (but don't move either hand) as you sing and name the pitch that is a 4th note above the root and then the 5th. If you need support, pluck the notes before singing them.

Not sure how to find the 4th? In the beginning, you may need to visualize playing a major scale and then count your way up, or find the 5th and come down a whole step. Another option would be to picture the major 3rd, if you're already familiar with it, and come up a half step. I call this *multiplex thinking*, meaning the ability to picture a number of passageways between notes simultaneously. Pianists and guitarists do this all the time because they're required to play more than one note at a time.

Each of the three notes we've just played is the root note to each of our three chords in the I- IV-V7

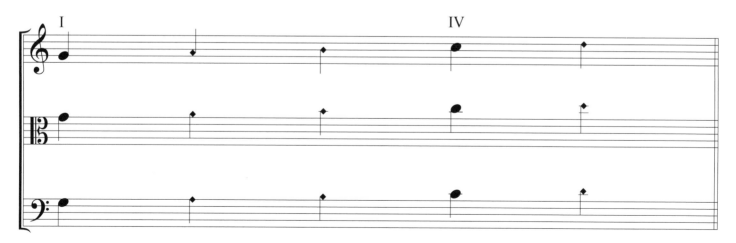

progression:

- G is the root of the I chord

- C is the root of the IV chord

- D is the root of the V chord

Now, we're going to play the roots again, but this time we'll add the major 3rd above each of them.

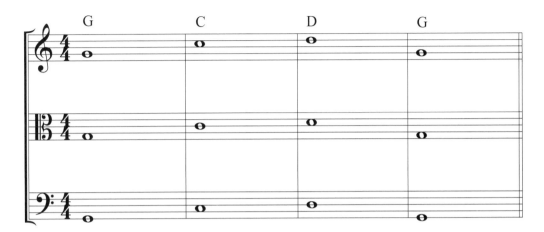

Let's add the perfect 5th on top:

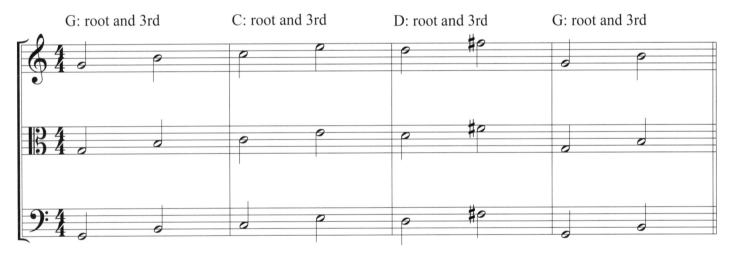

**Note:** Finding the 5th above each root note is easy. Our instruments are tuned in 5ths. Just picture the

finger that plays the root note (or open string) and move it straight across to the next higher string.

Now add the octave to the I and IV chords, but use the ♭7th for the V chord. Why does this chord have a ♭7th? Called the *dominant 7th chord*, its job is to steer our ears back home to the I chord. In this case, the F♯ in the D7 chord leads our ears to the G. And the C♮ in the D7 chord creates a tension that is resolved when we return home.

## What Do Chords Have to Do with Soloing?

When the rhythm section plays each chord, you will dip into the arpeggio notes and scale tones prescribed by that chord as your resource for soloing. For instance, when the band plays the G chord, you'll be using notes from the G major arpeggio and scale. Likewise, you'll use the notes of the C major arpeggio and scale for the IV chord. The D chord will be a little different: The scale is called the Mixolydian mode because it's a major scale with a ♭7th and the V chord, as we've discussed above, is called a dominant 7th chord.

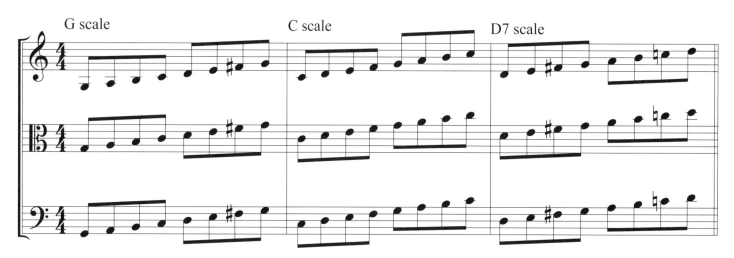

Now that you've practiced finding the primary tones and scales of each of our three chords, the next logical step is to make your solo different and interesting every time you play across this progression. Think back across all the skills we've covered: rhythmic and pitch permutations, patterns, and ornamentation. These are the tools you have worked to master by this stage in your progression through this book; they are sufficient to create a diverse and interesting solo.

**Note:** You could get away with playing in G major all the way across the progression outlined above and, give or take a note here and there, sound perfectly fine. So why bother with the practice techniques you've just worked on? Soloing with seven notes would eliminate the possibility of arpeggios on each of the chords; the more tools you have in your back pocket, the more interesting you'll sound.

**What Do I Do Next?**

Apply the exercises above to all 12 keys and then you'll be ready for anything and everything. If this seems overwhelming, keep in mind that one key a week across the I-IV-V7-I progression would take three months. Need more time? One key a month would take a year. That's well worth the work since, as we've discussed, playing with other musicians at a jam session or in a band requires being ready for whatever keys the other musicians prefer.

## The ii-V7-I Progression

 **II-V7-I CHORD PROGRESSION IN G**

The ii-V7-I is another popular chord progression you will come across. It is well worth preparing for this progression in all 12 keys. We will work on it in the key of C because it will help you understand this progression more easily.

Since the ii chord is minor, as indicated by lower-case Roman numerals (Dm in this case), the 3rd and 7th are flatted. For this example, D major loses its two sharps, and the dominant 7th symbol on the V7 chord (the G chord) strips that key of its only sharp. This means the three chords boil down to one single scale: the major scale built on the root note. I call it "a whole lot of hullabaloo about nothing."

chordal scale for ii        chordal scale for V7        chordal scale for I chord

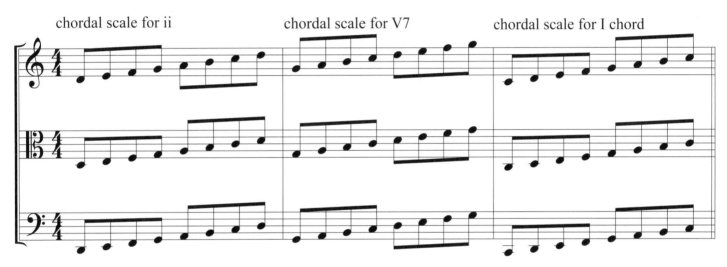

But imagine a melody with only one chord played over and over again to accompany it. How boring would that be? This chord sequence brings color and energy to the accompaniment of a melody extremely rooted in its key signature, at least for the section of the tune the progression is applied to. And you may well wonder, "Why should I bother cooking my brain cells over a progression that can boil down to a single scale?" It's because you will start to bore yourself if you keep soloing using only one scale—in this case, the C major scale. The chords provide many pathways on your fingerboard because the arpeggio for each chord can be used to create a more interesting solo. The time you spend learning the chord tones in this progression will help you generate a richly diverse solo.

Your goal will be to think a chord and instantly visualize its chord and scale tones across your instrument. To prepare, make sure you include the "Pitch Permutation" work introduced earlier in this unit, by practicing scrambling each chord's four notes in every possible order. In other words, you don't want to be in the middle of a solo, hear the V7 chord coming up, and automatically hit its root note every single time; you want all options available at all times.

## What Do I Do With All the Other Chords?

Since my other books, namely *Improvising Violin* and *The Contemporary Violinist*, cover this material, I will not go into detail here. In general, it's important to keep in mind that there are seven basic chord types; each chord symbol tells the player what kind of arpeggio and scale to build off its root note.

Some tunes provide an opportunity to solo using only one scale. while others require a thoroughly detailed chord-by-chord preparation.

There are some chord progressions I've worked on every day for decades to continue to build facility. I don't share this to discourage you, but rather to reassure you that if you have trouble playing on more complex tunes, you shouldn't assume that means anything negative about you and your skills. Some keys, chords, scales and progressions are more demanding than others. It's up to you to do the necessary work.

Here is a quick overview of the chords you'll encounter the most often. I suggest you memorize the chord tones first for each primary chord. Organize your practice sessions to cover one key at a time, moving to a new key only when you can sing, name, visualize, and play the present key with certainty and good intonation.

### BASIC CHORD TYPES

| Name | Symbol | Chord Tones |
|------|--------|-------------|
| Major | $\Delta$ | 1, 3, 5, 7 |
| Dominant 7th | 7 | 1, 3, 5, $\flat$7 |
| Minor | - | 1, $\flat$3, 5, $\flat$7 |
| Diminished | $\circ$ | 1, $\flat$3, $\flat$5, $\flat\flat$7 |
| Augmented | + | 1, 3, $\sharp$5, $\flat$7 |

# HOW CAN I INDIVIDUALIZE MY SOUND?

We can all agree that basic technique is required to play a piece of music, no matter what the style. Quite simply, if you don't know how to hold your bow, how can you generate tone or rhythm? If you don't know how to position your left hand, how can you formulate melodies? Therefore, each system, with the exception of learning via ear and eye in a fiddling community, accepts and subscribes to the fact that every single student will learn to play the exact same exercises and pieces in the exact same order. Examples include my first violin teacher Samuel Applebaum's *String Builder* series, on through a range of pedagogies worldwide, to the internationally accepted Suzuki method.

Why do so many string teachers accept this cookie-cutter training process so complacently without tailoring exercises and musical choices to the individual? Because it's efficient to rely on a time-tested method since a great deal of thought and study pertaining to how we learn has been incorporated into each system.

But there comes a moment in every player's life—unless he or she opts for the role of interpretative artist within a chamber ensemble or orchestra, or guardian of a specific roots tradition—when it becomes imperative to develop a personal voice on his or her instrument.

So how do we accomplish this, having evolved from a method-dominated or tradition-heavy approach to learning? Is it possible to teach technique such that we emerge able to teach ourselves—and, of course, our students—how to evolve our own unique thumb print? Aside from personal choices like the style(s) of music that best suits personal taste, type of tone or vibrato, tempo and mood preferences, this really boils down to a question of phrasing, expression, and embellishment.

> "Be yourself; everyone else is already taken." Is your credo based on the Oscar Wilde quote, or is it based on a desire to fit into a preexisting mold?

For those of you wishing to develop a unique voice or to teach others how to achieve this, here are a few steps that can help.

## Learning from a Respected Artist

You may wonder how the study of a known player's signature sound might help you develop your own. The distinction is this: We aren't trying to imitate, but to learn from. This is an entirely different approach to ear training.

The idea here is to learn and then analyze a solo or tune from the artist who best exemplifies the style or sound you admire, to gain an understanding of how he or she forged a recognizable footprint in the string world. If possible, notate the solo and then break your analysis down into individual elements, such as:

- Preferred rhythms and/or rhythmic phrases

- Where and how rests are applied within the flow of playing

- Dynamics

- Note choices within or outside the basic melody, key signature, or chord changes.

On the next page, you'll find a phrase from a solo by legendary jazz violinist Claude "Fiddler" Williams. I like to ask myself questions like, "Are the notes sustained or clipped?" And, "If a note is cut short, is it by lifting up out of the note or digging in? And by what degree?" Then I might analyze pitch choices against the chords the band is playing to try to hear how that artist hears. I'm also interested in tone, expressiveness, accentuation, and anything else my ears can discern.

**CLAUDE "FIDDLER" WILLIAMS**

When I examine another artist's solo, I try to apply my discoveries to my own solos any way I can. For instance, from this excerpt, I'm particularly interested in how "Fiddler" starts by arpeggiating in E♭ and then chooses notes outside the chord changes before tucking back into chord tones by the time he reaches the C minor chord. His choices create tension and spice. His placement of accents, syncopation and slices of silence help build the integrity of his phrasing. That's a lot of information for the few measures we've spotlighted from his solo.

Next, I might take the idea that intrigues my ears the most and move that idea through the 12 keys, first chromatically and then moving down through the Cycle of Fifths. Why down through 5ths? Because that's the most common chord progression employed by most styles: church music, blues, swing, jazz, folk, Latin, and pop/rock.

**Note:** Moving down the interval of a 5th is equal to moving up the interval of a 4th. See "The 12-Key Challenge" in the "Practice Techniques" unit.

Then I might ask, "Does he ornament any of his notes?" In this case, there's a bluesy slide from the ♭3 of C up into the major 3rd, and he also applies chromatic motion leading up into his next idea. Then I invent a practice segment that runs those ideas through all 12 keys. For instance, the ♭3 of every key up into its major 3rd.

Let's look at a different example in another style to illustrate how much we can learn from just one point of focus—ornamentation.

Here's an example of the first few measures of the traditional Irish tune "Mountain Road." In the first version, I've sketched out only the basic pitches and rhythms so you can compare this to the unique interpretations each of two fiddlers has added to the same few measures.

**Note:** This example has been transposed down a 5th to accommodate viola and cello.

Next, we see the player in version one applied slurs in surprising places. Each change in bow direction helps highlight certain notes above others within the measure. In version two, we also see variations on the melody using turns and note substitutions.

## Connecting to Your Inner and Outer Voice

Your voice can become your greatest asset. Try singing an improvisation. It doesn't matter if you sing out of tune. Just have fun and practice exploring different rhythmic and melodic motifs against a backing track. This will provide a direct connection between you and your muse without the physical constraints about how to navigate your instrument, or the expectations you've developed about the sounds you "should be able to generate" from your instrument.

## Maximizing Your Own Flashes of Inspiration

Let's take a completely different approach to individualizing your sound. Try improvising freely over a backing track. When you stumble across a new idea you like, use it.

- Analyze it.

- Isolate the right-hand motion and practice it on open strings.

- Move the idea through 12 keys.

- Move the idea up and down the fingerboard.

- Try to develop some spin-off ideas.

For instance, one day while soloing on my Flamenco piece "Harmonic Gypsy" (see *The Contemporary Violinist* distributed by Hal Leonard), I stumbled across a simple little idea of adding a string crossing to a rhythmic pattern.

Stumble was the key word here. Not only did I find the idea accidentally, but I did not execute it very well. So I stopped the accompaniment and isolated the bowing on open strings:

Then, it occurred to me that since alternated string crossing had shown up as a weakness in my technique, I should explore as many string crossing patterns as I could. After searching through hundreds of string recordings in numerous styles, I'm sad to say I didn't find many examples, so I borrowed a term from drummers, "paradiddles," to describe the practice series and came up with as many string crossing patterns as I could.

 **PARADIDDLES**

## 12 Paradiddles

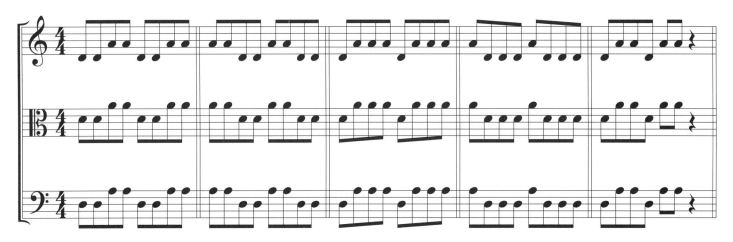

After practicing these paradiddles on open strings at various tempi against the metronome, add some left-hand patterns.

What ideas can you generate and develop to build your own individualized technique?

In the next section of this unit, "The Looper as a Creative Tool," you will find additional ideas about how to expand your creativity.

# THE LOOPER AS A CREATIVE TOOL

The looper is an electronic box that records everything you play. But, instead of recording to play back later, the looper immediately echoes what you've just played, repeating it over and over until you turn it off. And, while it's repeating your first idea, it's capable of recording a second idea that interlocks with the first, and then another and another. Depending on how sophisticated a unit you purchase, it is capable of recording loops from six beats on up to several hours.

In recent years the popularity of the looper has exploded on the music scene. When I do a school residency, it's well worth shipping out my amp beforehand and lugging my double violin case, cables, and stomp box. In years past, if I said anything like "We're going to work on creativity" or "I'm going to teach you how to improvise," I would see students' faces withdraw and gazes fall to the floor. Now, it takes only a minute to win them over wherever I go, no matter what the age group. When they hear the layers the looper allows me to record on the spot, I see total enthusiasm throughout the room. Yet, I'm teaching the same skills: How to manipulate pitch and rhythm to create original music.

Looping isn't new. Moving back through time, we find that almost every culture worldwide employs this musical device. Known as clave in Afro-Cuban music, ostinato (meaning "obstinate" in Italian) in classical, and riffs in Kansas City jazz, R&B, and blues, there are also many variations throughout African music.

A loop is like a Haiku poem. Short and to the point, it can convey a great deal of music in a brief unit of time. A really juicy idea begs to be repeated. You just can't get enough of it. In fact, many artists in American pop music have made their fortune with just one catchy riff. Examples that jump to mind include The Allman Brothers' "One Way Out," Cream's "Sunshine of Your Love," Jimi Hendrix's "Purple Haze," and Deep Purple's "Smoke on the Water." Not familiar with these examples? You can find them on the Internet.

> **Teachers:** You can use the looper to motivate your students to learn to compose and improvise without them even realizing it.

Preparation for, and the actual use of, the looper will improve a whole set of skills. This is because preparing to work with the actual device is a crafty way of working on composition and improvisation simultaneously, while developing the ability to fulfill every role required of a good ensemble: bass, rhythm, melody, and harmony. I have yet to find a single individual—no matter what age—who, once they see the looper in action, doesn't pine to get their hands on it and try it out.

## Six Ways to Fast-Track Your Skills Using a Looper

1) "Rhythmize" your bow: Think you can play on the beat? Think again. Using the looper will challenge everything you ever believed about your rhythmic skills, or even about playing on time across four beats. It will also enable you to improve those skills immeasurably.

2) Develop your compositional skills: There is an art to making music that is built on one- or two-measure interesting melodic/rhythmic musical ideas that interlock. It can be harder than it seems, but the effort is rewarded instantaneously and the learning curve is huge.

3) Hone your improvisational skills: Spontaneous composition requires the same skills as improvisation; invent and hear an idea in your inner ear and then externalize it on your instrument. The looper requires on-time delivery across a short, defined cycle of time. This makes more sense as a learning tool than challenging yourself or a student to improvise over a 12-bar blues or a 32-bar jazz tune when first starting to explore composition and improvisation. Looping is a microcosm of everything you'll need to be able to do within longer forms of music, but without the feeling of overwhelm.

4) Practice more: It's so much fun to stack loops and jam over them that time flies by.

5) Become an entire band: You (and your students) will learn how to be several different musicians at once: the bass player, the percussionist, the melodist, and the harmonist.

6) Improvise intonation and technique: The immediate feedback encourages on-the-spot corrections and adjustments; the repetitious nature of the activity helps improve bow right- and left-hand accuracy.

The good news is that you don't even need to buy the electronic box to get started. Let's explore some exercises you can apply as a player or teacher that will prepare or enhance skills for using the looper.

## Bass Lines

To use a looper effectively, you will need to learn to develop a bass line. The bass player supports the harmonic motion (the chords) of the tune while simultaneously articulating the rhythmic groove. His or her rhythmic choices will be determined by whether the tune is a rock song, jazz, Latin, or in a roots style like Appalachian or Klezmer. There are a number of ways to approach cultivating this skill. Here are a few:

### 1) Analytical

Let's look at a handful of bass lines over the I-IV-V7-I chord progression in the key of E major. Take a moment to study and compare how each bass line highlights and moves between the chord tones. Try playing through these to sample the subtle rhythmic differences between each line.

**Appalachian**

**Bluegrass**

**Pop Calypso**

**Classic Rock**

**'70s Soul**

Invite five bass players to play a bass line over the same chord structure and style, and no two will sound exactly the same. With this in mind, we can still learn a great deal about the role the bassist fulfills as a support to the rest of the band.

**Southern Gospel**

**Latin Bossa Nova**

**Klezmer**

**Blues**

Now try to write your own bass line over this same chord sequence:

### 2) Auditory

Select a recording in a style you like. If need be, slow the recording down. Try to learn at least four measures of the bass line from the recording by playing along and picking out notes and rhythms. Sometimes it's easier to grab this information with your voice first, and then transfer it to your instrument.

Don't worry if you find this difficult, particularly if you're a violinist or fiddler, since your ears are more accustomed to picking out the higher melody line. With a little bit of practice, your ears will learn to identify the pitches and rhythms from the bass player.

Optional: Using the I-IV-V7-I audio accompaniment in E, generate a series of bass lines using pizzicato or arco keeping the examples we've just surveyed in mind.

 **II-V7-I CHORD PROGRESSION IN E**

### 3) Improvisational

Here's another approach to working on these same skills:

- Select a recording of a tune in a style you like, or record yourself playing a tune.

- Play with the recording. Just noodle around and search for a few notes that sound good. This will also help you locate the key signature. If you don't like how a note sounds, move around until you find a few notes that are agreeable.

- Using the notes you've found, develop a repetitious pattern that sounds good, adding a rhythmic feel to how you bow them.

- Add *chromatic* (half step) or *diatonic* (scale-like) passing tones to travel between the chord tones.

## Harmony

There is no right or wrong way to develop a harmony part for a melody. It's a matter of taste. Here are a few steps you can experiment with to get started:

1) Choose a recording you like. Find one note that sounds good against it. Hold it like a drone, or apply a rhythmic figure to it. That's your first harmony part.

2) Working with that same recording, figure out how to play a phrase of the melody. Then try to create a parallel line that mirrors the rhythmic and melodic motion. For instance, you could play a 3rd above, a 6th below… or any other interval above or below the melody line. That's your second harmony part.

3) Now try to create a parallel line that doesn't always agree rhythmically, and vary the interval distance between the melody and your harmony. There's your third harmony part!

Here are a few examples:

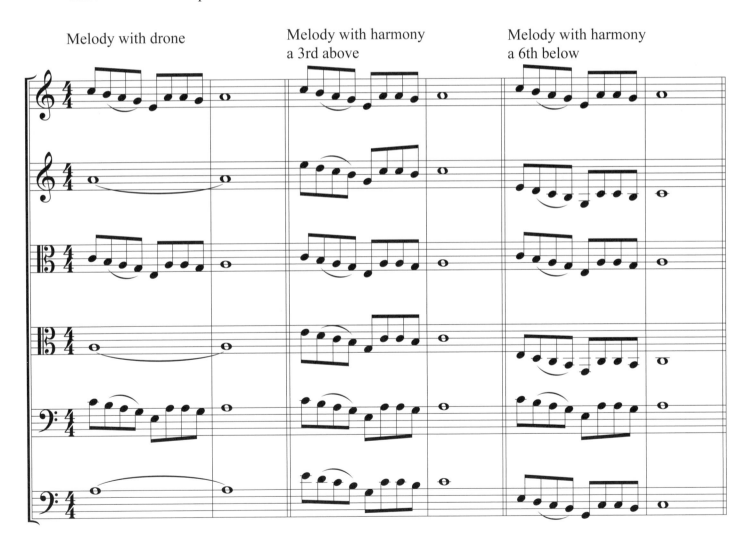

Melody with drone      Melody with harmony a 3rd above      Melody with harmony a 6th below

Melody with harmony an octave above  Melody with mixed rhythms and harmony notes  Melody with mixed rhythms and harmony notes

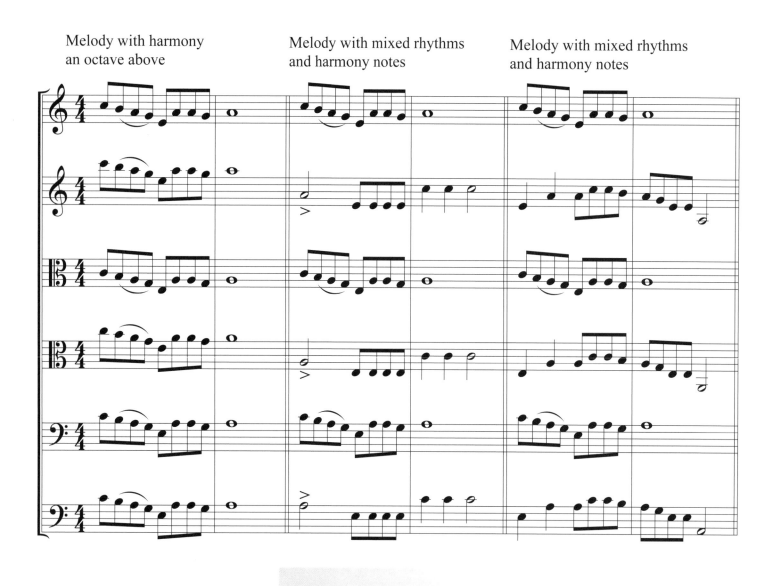

## Playing Rhythm

▶ PLAYING RHYTHM

Hearing, feeling, and playing with a percussionist's ears doesn't always come naturally to string players, but it's a handy skill to develop. You will be able to use this capability when layering loops, as well as when jamming with others or while playing tunes and melodies.

First, you will have to temporarily subdue your melodic ears. To accomplish this, choose one or two notes and focus exclusively on your bow. The point is to think simple and pretend your bow is really a drumstick. Since string players tend to focus a great deal more on the left hand—to tune every note and carry out the melody—you will benefit from time spent focused only on your right hand and the development of your rhythmic vocabulary.

Here are steps you can take to practice putting a rhythmic groove together:

- Play four quarter notes across two measures in 4/4.

- Replace the first quarter note in each measure with one of the options pictured below.

- Replace the second quarter note in each measure with another option.

- Choose rhythmic substitutions for the third, and then the fourth, quarter note.

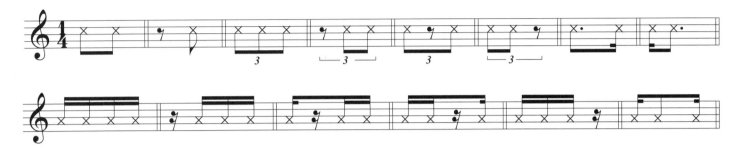

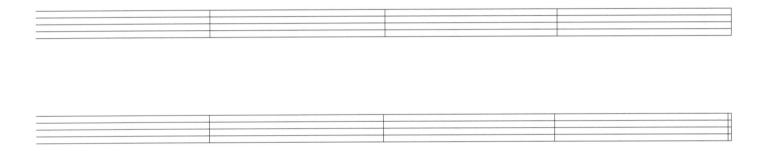

See? That wasn't difficult. Do you feel like you were cheating? Well, you weren't. We just used visual instead of aural information to walk you through a step-by-step process. Do you have to limit yourself to the rhythmic options outlined above? No.

- Write out some new rhythmic options in the blank staff or figure them out on your instrument.

- Now, repeat the process and use your own rhythmic ideas as options.

- Repeat the process again, but this time close your eyes and turn to your ears to supply you with possible substitutions.

Remember the exercise "Rhythmic Permutations," way back in the unit titled "Practice Techniques"? It will be helpful to review that exercise, because the skills that will serve you most when playing rhythm will include the interaction of accents and rests with interesting time values. Try repeating the exercises outlined above. This time, add accents, rests, and/or clipped notes.

Try all the exercises listed above at the frog, using short bows moving the bow in the shape of a smile. When the bow hits the string, that's the bottom of the smiley shape; the rest of the time, the bow is in the air.

You can also apply standard classical techniques such as *staccato* (a sequence of short on-the-string bows using a bow-stroke called *martelé*), *spiccato* (bounced bow), *tremolo* (a fast up and down shimmer at the tip of the bow), or *chop technique* (a textural rhythm generated at the frog of the bow).

## The Art of the Riff

As previously mentioned, after many decades teaching improvisation one-on-one, as well as to huge groups of students in school residencies, I've come to the conclusion that the most potent route any musician can take to building excellent improvisational skills is to work with a looper—or at least prepare to work with one.

The ability to generate a short melodic/rhythmic phrase, and then remember and repeat it, can tap into and help develop a number of key skills for improvisation:

- Composition: an awareness of a beginning, middle and end

- Creativity: the ability to generate a musical idea extemporaneously

- Auditory memory: the ability to hear, play, and memorize an impromptu musical phrase

- Time sequence recognition: the ability to hear and feel an exact number of beats and generate a musical phrase that honors that time increment

- Harmony: repetition of a short melodic phrase enables the player to work on hearing and playing a harmony part extemporaneously

- Ensemble techniques: the ability to create a short, interlocking musical phrase that works within an ensemble context

Western European composers across history constantly incorporated theme and variation into their works. When we scan music from around the globe, we find some cultures—like African and East Indian—include repetition as an important core ingredient to how they approach improvisation and composition. When players or students are inexperienced with either composition or improvisation, there is a tendency to build a melody that leans toward the constant generation of new musical ideas. In fact, themes are rarely repeated. The art of the riff, on the other hand, focuses on groove and repeatability, and provides you with an opportunity to hone these skills. Let's analyze two short melodic phrases. One qualifies as a riff while the other doesn't.

> Did you know that, aside from building great riffs to use with the looper, you can solo for as long as you want over the stacks of loops you record?

In the first example, the melody leads our ears to believe the first measure will be followed by another idea, and then another.

Using the same pitches, the second example is a self-contained unit that begs to be repeated.

It seems like an easy task to generate a catchy riff, doesn't it? Yet, it can be rather elusive. Here are some guidelines that will help:

- Choose a key.

- Choose a type of scale (major, minor, modal, ethnic).

- Choose a four- or eight-beat time increment.

- Choose a start note and an ending note, preferably derived from or designed to revolve around the chord tones in that key: the root, 3rd, or 5th.

Put on a drum machine or create a backing track. See: "Technology for Strings: How to Generate Your Own Backing Tracks."

- Add some pitches in between the start and end notes.

- Add some rhythmic ideas to the phrase to spice it up.

Here's an example that follows these guidelines. First, I've arbitrarily chosen a start and end note for my riff.

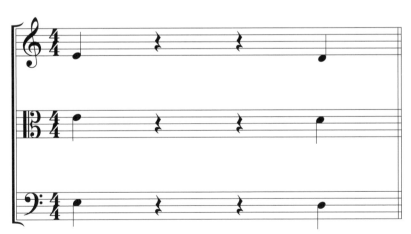

After some noodling, I chose the notes I wanted to work with and added rhythmic figures with a chromatic passing tone, and voilà, there's my latest riff. Notice how the final D naturally leads us back up to the beginning of the riff.

You might base your choices on:

- A key you feel most comfortable with

- Notes that might work well again a song your band is preparing for performance

- A handful of notes from a recording you particularly enjoy

Refer to the earlier sections on "Pitch Permutations" and "Rhythmic Permutations" to develop more note-to-note possibilities.

## The Looper Concept in an Acoustic Ensemble Setting

We can also prepare to use the looper acoustically in a group setting. The directions below have been worded for a string orchestra director, but you can also achieve these results with a few other musicians in a chamber music group, a band, or with friends.

This first exercise will require a drum machine if working with a larger group.

- Seat players in circles of four and explain that the group is going to become a looping machine.

- Invite each group to choose a group leader and to decide whether they will rotate clockwise or counterclockwise.

- Choose a key and a scale and familiarize the entire group with the notes. Then limit them to three or four notes to begin with, like the root, 3rd, 4th, and 5th of the key.

- Explain that when you count everyone in, after the drum machine or percussion backbeat has begun, the group leader will lay the bass line. If you haven't yet introduced them to this concept as outlined earlier in this unit, invite the leader to play as simple an idea as possible. Explain that the leader will keep repeating his or her loop.

- Invite each player in the group to layer in, one by one, with a repeating four-beat phrase until everyone is playing simultaneously. (The agreed-upon key and drum machine will produce a lovely full-group sound.)

- Try this step for a few minutes before motioning for silence. Then invite each player to change his or her idea each time the group finishes rotating around the circle to the leader. Voilà! Everyone is composing and improvising simultaneously.

This exercise works best if you can demonstrate a looper first. That's what gets folks excited. If you don't have this piece of equipment or know how to use it, find an example on YouTube (there are hundreds to choose from) and play that for everyone.

# Using the Looping Concept for Creative Conducting & Student Leadership

▶ **CREATIVE CONDUCTING & STUDENT LEADERSHIP**

So far, we have looked at a dozen or more different approaches to improvisation. There is an additional one I want to give you an opportunity to explore. You will need an ensemble to apply this approach. I have provided you with four different *flexi-scores* to work with. Flexi, meaning that the parts can be layered simultaneously many different ways, just like what we've already worked on in this section with the looper.

The numbers in each score provide a tool for layering these parts vertically, meaning each musical phrase was chosen for its ability to interlock and be performed simultaneously with the other phrases. If you're an individual, you can record the parts into your looper. If you're a string director, you go a lot further. It's simple: The conductor signals a group of players by holding up a number with his or her fingers, and conducts that group in on the downbeat. Each piece invites creative conducting on the part of the string director, students in the ensemble, or even the audience members if you opt to perform one of these flexi-scores. Whoever is conducting will generate a totally unique piece. This is because the piece will keep changing and evolving depending on the use of dynamics, how many parts are stacked simultaneously, how those parts combine, and so on.

The conductor can:

- Opt to cut out all but one player

- Layer everyone in on one part, two parts, or equally divided across all the parts

- Segregate parts by level to accommodate playing ability

- Work on original hand signals with the players to convey a range of directions that can include: dynamics, to play the same part up an octave or down an octave, switch to pizzicato and back to arco, add tremolo, or any other desired elements

- Individual or small-group solos over the background lines

This exercise combines student leadership (similar to taking a solo, but far safer for a beginner) with creativity. The parts are short enough to be memorized if you decide to include this in a performance. Or, you can also compose—or invite your students to—interlocking parts and use this approach as yet another way to create a giant looping machine, one that feels more secure since the students already know their parts.

I have provided you with four different pieces to work with. Each one is in a different style. There are numerous one-measure or two-measure parts that are numbered and can be layered by a single individual if you're using a looper or by a string orchestra. I call these flexi-scores because the outcome is always in a state of flux, and open to your imagination. You can add some of your own parts to any of these pieces.

> **String Teachers:** You are more than welcome to make copies of these scores for practice and performance. I hope that once you catch onto how I've generated the parts, you'll consider creating some pieces of your own or inviting your students to do so.

For this first flexi-score, I've borrowed some classic lines from the boogie-woogie style to build a group of stackable loops. This particular score provides a few additional opportunities. Here are the options for this piece:

- You can use the parts as written and record each layer into your looper.

- You can solo over the recorded layers in your looper.

- Earlier in the book we covered the I-IV-V pattern. You—or, if you're a string teacher, your students—can use this as an opportunity to transpose the parts up a 4th and up a 5th from the home key of C to practice moving each boogie-woogie part through the I-IV-V-I progression. For instance, here is the first boogie-woogie riff transposed through the I-IV-V chord changes:

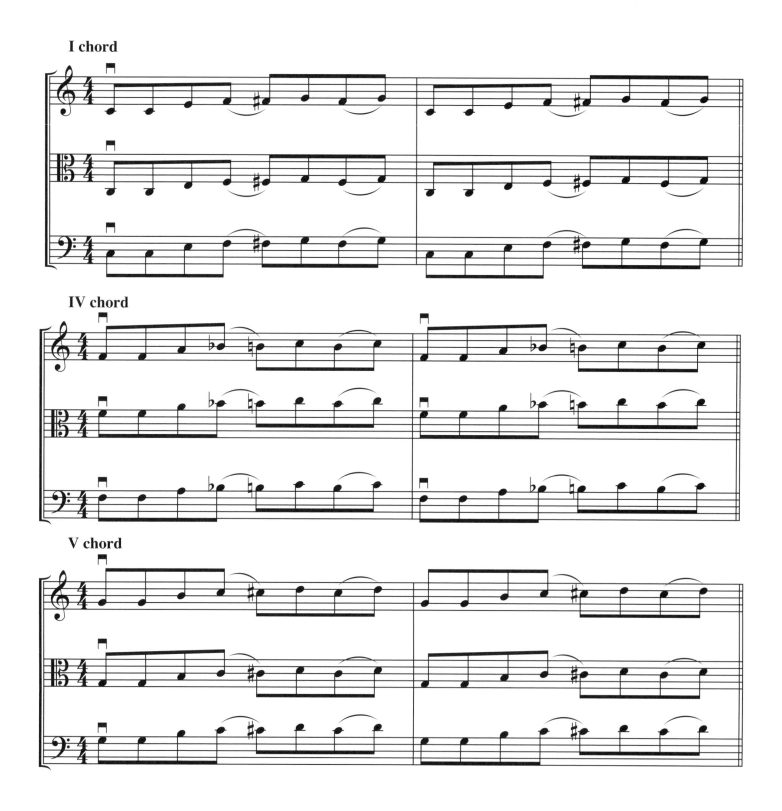

- Once the parts have been moved through the I-IV-V-I, that progression can be applied to the blues structure pictured below:

**I chord for four bars**

**IV chord for two bars**          **I chord for two bars**

**V chord for one bar**   **IV chord for one bar**   **I chord for two bars**

The first boogie-woogie hit was "Pinetop's Boogie Woogie" by Pinetop Smith, recorded in 1928 and first released in 1929. But the genre known as boogie-woogie first developed in the African-American community in the 1870s and then became popular in the 1920s. This tradition started out as a piano style and evolved into big band and even country and western music. Most boogie-woogie tunes are based on a driving eighth-note pulse in 4/4 time.

Even though boogie-woogie is not considered a bowed string player's style, if you read my book *Rockin' Out with Blues Fiddle*, you can learn more about how slave fiddlers and singers developed the art form we call "the blues." Since boogie-woogie is primarily based on the 12-bar blues form, we can assume this art form wouldn't have evolved without the earlier musical contributions made on violin.

**BLUES FIDDLER HOWARD ARMSTRONG**

# Boogie-Woogie Romp

# Kpanlogo

The parts to "Kpanlogo" (pronounced "panlogo") come from a traditional piece played on *gyli* (pronounced "jee-lee"), an African marimba from South Ghana. I was told by the American marimba player Valerie Naranja that the village plays this piece if something has been stolen. It's a gentle way to let everyone in the community know that the item should be returned to its owner. If not, the next night, the musicians might sing the name(s) of the suspect thief or thieves.

# Latin Jam

I've combined some fun Latin lines. It would be useful to listen to a few recordings of Afro-Cuban music to familiarize yourself with note-to-note phrasing. For instance, shortened notes (indicated by the dot above the note) should not be staccato. Abbreviate note length by decreasing bow pressure while stopping bow motion on the string.

# Bach Double

I combed through J.S. Bach's *Concerto for Two Violins, Strings, and Continuo in D Minor, BWV 1043* to find musical phrases that could be played simultaneously. I doubt Bach would mind if he were alive today, since he was a world-class improviser on the pipe organ.

Choose a classical piece of music and try extracting parts that can be layered for the looper or for string orchestra.

# What to Buy and How to Use the Looper

## Features and Procedures

Each company that makes and sells a looping machine has configured their machine slightly differently, so it would be impossible to give instructions that apply to every single looper on the market. However, there are certain features you need to know about—and what to look for—when shopping for a looper.

1) This machine is also known as a stomp box. You will control it with your foot so your hands are free to play your instrument.

2) You will need either a solid-body instrument or a pickup mic that has the capacity to plug into a stomp box using a quarter-inch guitar plug. You will also need an amp to hear the loops you record. (See the unit "Technology for Strings" for more information.)

3) If the stomp box is a dedicated looper or offers additional features, it has been configured to record a specific phrase length. The higher the price, the more recording time you'll get.

4) If looping capability is combined with other features, such as special effects, you may have only four to six beats available to you, but you will still be able to record a series of loops that plays back simultaneously.

5) More expensive loopers will provide you with the ability to delete specific loops while keeping others. This is no different than a recorder: Depending on its maker and configuration, every recording machine offers a certain number of independent tracks you can record on.

For instance, let's say you record the first phrase and really like it, you're okay with the second phrase, but the third phrase is especially interesting and now you decide to get rid of the second one. You would not be able to delete the middle phrase on an inexpensive machine or mixed-purpose stomp box, but you would have that capacity on a more expensive, dedicated looper.

6) Every looper comes with a button you can step on to stop the layers of loops from playing back; if held for a certain number of seconds, it will erase the loops you've recorded. Some units allow you to save your recording and move it to your computer.

7) You will need to learn how to coordinate one of your feet with both of your hands; otherwise, the loop will record and play back slightly cockeyed. This takes practice.

Here's an approach that will help you synchronize your new "third hand":

- Practice stepping on the "record" button on the downbeat. Make sure you wear shoes that are easy to work with. Sandals and flip-flops are problematic in this context.

- Next, practice drawing your first note in perfect unison with stepping on the button.

- Now play a four-beat phrase and pretend you are going to repeat the phrase. Just as you draw your bow on the beginning of the first note on the next downbeat, your foot must press the button again. This procedure will provide you with a clean loop. Repeat this procedure for each new loop.

## Which Looper Should I Buy?

Since the looper will sit on the floor, be sure the stomp box you purchase has a large enough LCD screen for you to read when you look down at it while standing. Read online reviews to search for comments like "I was able to use this looper just minutes after set-up." From reviewer's comments, you will also learn a lot about the various features available and how they work.

Ultimately, your budget will make the final decision for you, but you can always purchase last year's model on Ebay. Chances are good that it will be in fine condition and serve you for many years.

**Note:** You can also use inexpensive apps on your smart phone or tablet that perform the same tasks as the stomp box. However, unless the app offers a foot pedal that can be ordered, you will have to coordinate your hands to move quickly back and forth between your device and your instrument. See "Technology for Strings."

# PLAYING IN A BAND

# GETTING STARTED

There are two types of bands: instrumental only or instrumental with featured vocalist(s). Every band has different goals, but there are some helpful pointers you can apply to ensure your success working with other musicians.

This unit is going to assume we are discussing an ensemble dedicated to either a traditional roots style, a combination of styles, a rock/pop group, and/or creative styles of music like blues, swing, jazz, or originals.

Over the years, I've seen a lot of groups with high hopes disband after a short period of time. Time and again, this occurs because certain steps weren't taken at the beginning of the rehearsal process. I've also worked with a number of frustrated string players who were originally paper-trained and then found themselves in a band of musicians who rehearsed and played everything by ear.

Many string players find out during their first few rehearsals that the members of the band—particularly the leader (usually the vocalist, but not always)—often don't know anything about chords, keys, or structural elements. The bandleader tends to create songs by ear and then work out arrangements with the *rhythm section* (guitar, keyboard, bass, and drums) through trial and error. For this reason, asking for help from the leader won't always produce useful results. The rhythm section is usually able to be more helpful, but not invariably. This is why it's important to be prepared with your own procedures, so you can feel confident and play well.

When I recorded with pop icon Laura Nyro on her last album before her death, *Mother's Spiritual*, her instructions consisted of statements like, "Can you play with a little more green in your sound?" The engineer waved frantically from behind her to silence me when I asked what key the first song was in, and sometimes she would just sing a line she wanted me to use (in a different key from the recording) and expect me to grab it after one pass and magically transfer it into the correct key, as if I could psychically tune in to where and how she wanted it applied to the song. I had always loved her music, and even though this was a one-time gig for a recording—and an honor to work with her—I have no doubt that had I toured with her, things wouldn't have been tremendously different.

Here are some things you can do—when appropriate to the situation—to help you build success:

- Discuss and plan the role that you, the bowed string player, will fulfill within the group. Depending on the style, you might be responsible for melody, pads, fills, rhythmic backup, and/or solos. We have already covered a few of these topics in this book, but you'll find more information in this chapter.

- Be clear about time commitments, who is in charge of what, where you will meet to rehearse, and how the group will handle lateness, lack of preparation, or cancellation. These are issues that can ruin the potential to co-create wonderful music.

- Be clear about the rehearsal process. Whether the group works by ear or uses charts or scores, it's important to have a system in place to keep track of agreements about the arrangements for each piece. There's nothing worse than getting onstage and first discovering that each member of the group remembers a different version of who does what.

- If you will be playing by ear—with no written roadmaps—and intend to solo or generate harmony parts, you will need to determine the tonal map that best suits each piece of music.

**Listen and look for:**

- Tonal center

- Type of scale

- Favored intervals in the style

- Favored rhythmic motifs

- Meter

- Tempo

- Structure

- Unison versus harmony

- Ornamentation (left- and right-hand)

- Arrangement

- Underlying rhythmic groove

- Phrasing (length of each idea, entrances and exits)

- Dynamics

- Person-to-person onstage interaction

## Finding the Tonal Map

Whether you know nothing or a great deal about music theory, and in particular, playing over chord changes, apply an ears-first method. If a note sounds bad, avoid it. Start simple and gradually add notes into your map. You may end up with only five notes on up to more than seven. If you want to keep a journal, record each rehearsal with the group's permission and then sketch out a schematic for every song or piece at home.

Since standing anonymously behind a music stand in this context during performance conveys the look of an amateur, consider devising an abbreviated system of cues linked to specific lyrics or the overall form of each piece of music. You can place cue cards on the floor in front of you or on an amp nearby.

**Possible cue sheet for blues tune:**

Notice how the entire 12-bar country blues form can be written on less than one line, instead of using staff paper:

4x: E7//// 2xA7//// 2x: E7//// B7//// A7//// 2x: E7////

If you are already comfortable working with chord changes, then determining the notes that will sound best will be easy when you look at a chart with chord symbols. If you aren't familiar with chords, try to glean a "hybrid scale" (a group of notes that works across the chord changes) by ear.

Normally, this will work best by using the scale tones suggested by the key signature while listening for notes to flat, sharp, or just plain avoid.

# MAPPING THE SONG

While instrumental tunes can vary, depending on the style, every song is made up of verses and something called "the bridge" or "the chorus." Easy to recognize, the chorus repeats a number of times throughout the song with the same lyrics and melody. The actual number of verses and choruses will vary from song to song.

To play well, you can organize information about each song after or during the first rehearsal with the band by generating a cue sheet for the band's repertoire. It could include:

- The names of the songs the band plays

- The key of each song

- The tempo (ballad, medium tempo, or up-tempo)

- The number of verses and choruses

- The role you will play within each song, which we will call a *Song-Map*

**A Song-Map might look something like this:**

"Fight the Power": Key of E, medium tempo

Uses six-note scale: E-F#-G-A-B-D-E

Three verses, three choruses, lead, and tag

Song opens with two-note vocal intro (echo it using A & B notes)

First verse: keep two-note phrase going, but change the rhythms; second verse: sit out; third verse: use cool rhythms on D, E, and F#

Tag: Sit out

**Note:** There is a jam section before third verse: use original two-note rhythm on A and B notes.

Pick a recording of a song or tune you like and try generating your own map. Use descriptions that make sense to you personally, making a note on this form of what you plan to play for each section. Then play along with the song while you use your map:

# My Song-Map

**Name of Song:**

**Tonal Center (key):**

**Pivotal Notes (or scale):**

**Tempo:**

**Number of Verses:**

**Number of Choruses:**

**Meter:**

**Verse I:**

**Verse II:**

**Verse III:**

**Chorus:**

**Solo:**

**Additional Notes:**

# DETERMINING YOUR ROLE

Depending on band leadership and agreements, you may stick to one role only, or fulfill a number of roles: melody, backup lines, soloing, or a mixture of all three. It's fine to experiment as a group, but best to work out who does what beforehand as discussed earlier. After all, you don't want to accidentally launch into a spellbinding fill when the guitarist has already started to play.

It's also great to mix things up and make sure each tune is arranged differently so the audience never knows what to expect.

## Pads, Fills, Leads, and Tags

Playing the melody is a no-brainer for bowed string players. If that's what you and the band prefer, so be it. But this is an opportunity to challenge yourself and foster new skills.

### Pads

These are long tones that complement the melody. If you don't have the technique to play harmonies using double stops, you might opt to use a harmonizer, a stomp box effect that doubles each note you play. You can tune it to add a 6th below, a 3rd above, or an octave below to fatten your sound.

### Fills

A fill is a tasty line that's woven between breaks in the lyrics or in between featured melodic lines when another instrument is playing melody. It's important to familiarize yourself with the lyrics and melody so you can navigate smoothly. If your band has a singer, then lyrics take center stage—understandably so. The violin in particular will tend to compete with the singer's voice, so using fills is an excellent device to complement featured moments within the arrangement.

When playing fills or soloing, you can use the melody in a number of ways:

- Echo the melody an octave higher or lower.

- Use the melody notes, but change the order with which you play them or change their rhythmic phrasing.

- Add a few chromatic passing tones or ornaments to the scale.

### Rhythmic Backup

Whether it's tremolo, spiccato, chop technique, a rhythm you pick up from the bass, keyboard, or guitar, or rhythmic patterns you've invented, using your bow like a drummer's mallet with simple left-hand motion can help glue the band together and generate a solid groove for the audience to enjoy.

### Soloing

Predetermine a spot in the song that will give you an extended moment to shine out. The skills developed by practicing techniques outlined throughout this book will help you generate ideas to use for your solo. Try to focus on telling a story with your solo, much the way the singer has with the lyrics (if there is a singer in your group). This is also a good time to play on your higher strings so your instrument sails out above the band.

# WHAT COMES BEFORE AND WHAT GOES AFT?

Things can get pretty boring if every tune or song is counted in with "One, two, three, four…" You can cook up a *lead* (introduction) or a *tag* (ending) to help diversify the arrangements of pieces in each set.

Leads and tags are usually two or four bars (measures) in length. They must be built on the notes from the key. While there are no steadfast rules to what does and doesn't work, there are some basic guidelines you can use to help you get started.

### Leads or Kick-Offs

Leads often—but not always—start on the "and" of the beat on a note other than the tonic (the root of the key), and end on the 5th of the key to segue into the tune or song. This creates anticipation and tension, which is then resolved once the main body of the song launches.

Here's the opening to a fiddle tune I will use for some additional examples:

Familiarize yourself with the melody before you take a look at three possible two-bar leads. This first example opens with a fairly close mirror of the melody.

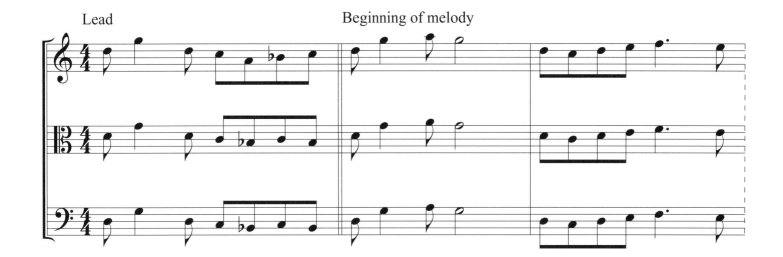

In this second example, I've mirrored the melody a little bit differently. The line does its job: It leads into the melody quite nicely. But my rhythmic choices are problematic. There aren't any 16th-note figures throughout the song. I've misled the listener to expect a fast note-to-note motion the tune never delivers.

In this third example, the lead isn't related to the melody, but it's made up of notes from the key.

You can echo an important rhythmic element in the melody or something the rhythm section is playing to accompany the song; or you can play something entirely different. In any case, choose a rhythm or rhythmic phrase that builds a feeling of anticipation as demonstrated above.

Some leads are stylized templates; they're used by players in that genre on a regular basis. For instance, here's a *kick-off*, as it's called in bluegrass/country music. I've heard this one a number of times over the years. It's played at the frog.

Try to write out a couple of your own one- or two-bar introductions to a tune that's in your repertoire. If notation isn't your forte, make them up by ear.

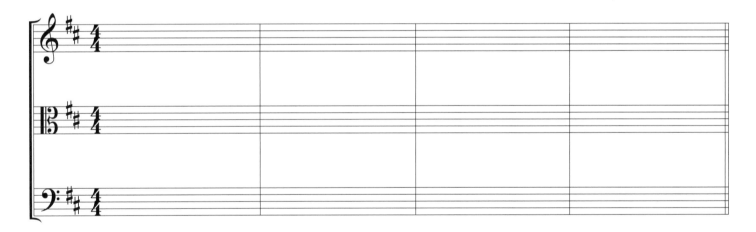

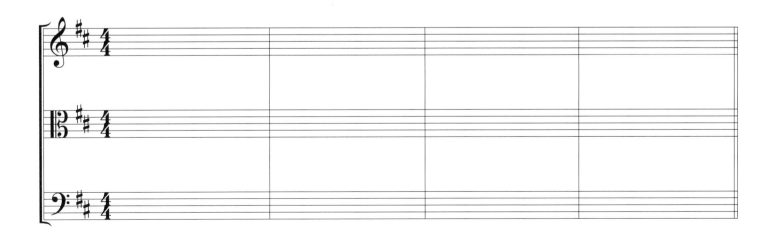

## Tags

Most tags end on the tonic, but that doesn't have to be the case. You might choose a note that makes the piece feel unfinished or that teases the audience. Remember the fiddle tag we used earlier in the book when we were working on variations on a melody? Well, let's revisit that line.

In each of the following four examples, I've opted for a different note with which to end the tag, and a different twist to head into that note. As you play each version, keep track of the sounds you like or don't like. Your preferences, if noted, will guide your choices in the future.

Now try a couple of your own. Use the Fiddle Tag audio for support.

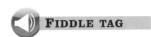 **FIDDLE TAG**

JULIE'S "STRINGS FOR NEWTOWN" CONCERT WITH MARK O'CONNOR, BRUCE MOLSKY, JAY UNGAR & MOLLY MASON, DONNA HEBERT; THE NORWALK YOUTH SYMPHONY; RICHARD BROOKS, CONDUCTOR

# RECORDING WITH YOUR GROUP

Nowadays, the bass line and chords are normally recorded first; the melody or vocals, as well as solos, are added in afterward. Your group will need to discuss this and make a decision about it. You may choose to record as a group in-studio or in performance, to capture a more spontaneous, interactive feel for the outcome. The in-studio method can sometimes produce rather sterile or controlled results.

Be prepared to spend a great deal of time getting set up for the recording, sometimes as much as the recording session itself. It's worth it. Make sure your headphones provide a sound that will enable you to relax while you play. Not all engineers understand how to set up sound for bowed string players. When in doubt, turn down the treble to ten or eleven o'clock and add a little reverb for ambience. While the engineer will record your sound without these enhancements and then set up the EQ (tonal settings) for the final sound during the mix later on, be certain you like what you hear through the headphones. If you can't stay afterward for the entire mix down, at least stay long enough to make sure you're happy with the sound.

To date, string players have played two completely different roles in rock music.

1) Anonymous string sections or soloists hired to record and perform using classical techniques. These string sections do not improvise or make original contributions to the music. They are considered "works for hire," and stay seated in the background. Basically, any skilled, well-trained string player can fulfill this role because it involves reading parts that the arranger for the band has written.

2) String soloists who have developed a vocabulary of traditional and contemporary techniques. These players also know how to play rhythm, use slide technique and textures, vary their vibrato or leave it out, and can improvise solos that bring the audience to its feet.

## Emotion

We've covered a lot about the mechanics that support playing with a group, but let's not forget the most important aspect of all: emotion. No matter how well you play, if your attention is only on skill and not on the emotions behind the music, your audience will most likely feel something is missing.

Be sure to read the unit "Cinematic Music" to work on conveying music through all your senses. Try thinking of emotion—along with color, sound, smell, and touch—as a range of energetic vibration that each of our senses has been configured to read and receive.

I once saw a singer in a class I was taking refuse to sing for the class because he'd been scheduled to sing a love song and was feeling incensed about something that had happened in his private life. Our teacher forced him to perform, and it was the most moving love song I'd ever heard. Anger, love, sorrow, compassion… these are all energetic states you can experiment with. Forge your own method for acting as a conduit for these emotions on your instrument.

## Stage Presence

When you stand onstage with a band, you will have to shake off the impression of the anonymous artist who's expected to disappear behind his or her instrument or music stand.

Now is the time to explore your individuality.

• What makes you different and special?

• How can you convey who you are when you play?

I'm not referring just to the music you play, but to how you look, how you stand, how you move while you play, and how you interact with the other musicians onstage.

Can you imagine going to a rock concert and watching the lead guitarist or singer stand perfectly still, while looking down at a music stand? Exactly.

Rehearse in front of a mirror or video camera so you can gain a clearer sense of the transition from introvert to extrovert. You may have to go overboard at first to break out of any awkwardness or embarrassment you might feel, but it's well worth the effort. The art of performance is about communicating with one's audience and sharing the gift of music. In addition, today's musician faces an audience that's accustomed to media. They are looking for visuals as much as sound; the element of surprise—even if just through changes in body position moment to moment—is an important tool you can use to engage attention.

## The Chemistry of Nervousness

Your sympathetic nervous system can't tell the difference between a tiger and an audience. It's been configured for survival, so your body will pump out over 20 different chemicals designed to deal with the "fight or flight response." That's because this is our body's primitive, automatic, inborn reaction that prepares the body to "fight" or "flee" from perceived attack, harm, or threat to our survival.

First, stop taking everyone's temperature, meaning stop wondering what everyone is thinking about you. Even if you asked each person, they probably wouldn't tell you or know themselves since we think many thoughts across each minute. Focus on hearing the music and your intent for your performance.

Second, reasoning with yourself ("It's just a group of people who love music." or "This isn't like it's the first time I've ever performed.") won't achieve anything. That's because the sympathetic nervous system doesn't respond to words. It will, however, respond to images. Here are a few that clients of mine have invented in the past to deal with stage fright. What works for one person may not work for another. You have to experiment until you find a personal solution.

1) "I imagined there was a shower curtain onstage and mentally pulled the curtains shut before I stepped out there. As I walked onto the stage, my heart rate quickened and I began to shake and sweat, but when I stepped behind my imagined curtain, I felt safe and stopped shaking. I was able to play better than I ever had before."

2) "I always feel as if I can't breathe when I'm offstage and am about to perform. I either find myself constantly yawning or trying to take a breath and feeling as though I can't. This time, I closed my eyes and pretended the air around me was my favorite color, green. Then I imagined sipping green air into my lungs. I pictured the color spreading down my arms, my torso, and my legs. I suddenly felt calm and noticed I was breathing deeply without any effort. The yawning stopped."

3) "My bow arm always shakes when I'm nervous, so I imagined it was made of light, flexible rubber. Even though I was still shaking, my bow stopped stuttering on the string."

# A FEW ADDITIONAL TIPS

## Onstage Sound

Since most start-up bands can't afford an engineer working sound at gigs, it's beneficial to have your own monitor and a preamp to hear yourself clearly and have control over your tone and volume. (See the unit "Technology for Strings.") This can consist of a small amp on a chair behind you or facing you, unless you're playing through a mic, which can generate feedback. In that case, angle the mic so it faces slightly away from where you'll be standing. It's also helpful to have a volume pedal so you can boost or lower your volume as needed with your foot while playing.

## Working with Vocalists

Vocalists tend to choose keys that are most comfortable to their vocal range. Make sure you are prepared to play in each and every one of the 12 keys. You want to be ready for all possibilities. You might be playing with friends right now, but you never know who will hear you and what opportunities might come your way. I like actor Denzel Washington's credo: "Luck is being in the right place at the right time and being prepared."

If you're invited to play behind the singer rather than just in between the lines, try to keep your lines supportive either by harmonizing with the melody or by providing simple repetitive phrases that mesh with the rhythmic values of the rest of the band. If you can't hear or understand the lyrics while you're playing, that's a sign your lines are too busy or too loud.

## People Politics

Whether playing in an instrumental or a vocalist-led band, be prepared for people politics. As is the case with any group of people, there will be differences in opinion, band members who are ethical and responsible and ones who aren't. Some individuals may even unintentionally echo their dysfunctional family history through how they interact with the people in the band. The firmer the agreements up front, the better the success for the group. These agreements must obviously include musical and professional goals, rehearsal protocol, as well as expectations around communication, preparation, and punctuality.

## Listen as a Policy

Listening means more than simply knowing what and when you're supposed to play. Listen to every instrument in the band, not just your own. Listen to the audience. Listen for dynamics. Listen for ideas before you play them. Listen to what you've just played to continue to improve. And listen for silence. If there's isn't any, make sure you add some. I like the way sculptor Henry Moore described how he approached a piece of marble, that the acknowledgment of the absence of material was as powerful as the form itself.

# TECHNOLOGY FOR STRINGS

🎵 **Why Learn About Technology for Strings?**

🎵 **Amplification and Special Effects**

🎵 **How Do I Choose What to Buy?**

🎵 **How to Create Your Own Backing Tracks**

🎵 **Recording and Arranging**

🎵 **Cinematic Music for Strings**

# WHY LEARN ABOUT TECHNOLOGY FOR STRINGS?

Many string players associate the use of an electric instrument with playing rock and pop music, but an amplified instrument can be used for any style of music. It can also open up a number of new musical and learning opportunities.

For instance, there's a lot of gear that even a dedicated acoustic string player can take advantage of. This section of the book will provide you with information on:

- How amplification can be used to enhance technique and musicianship

- Amplification options

- Hardware options, like the preamp, amp, or special-effects stomp box

- Software options like apps for smartphone and tablet, and software programs for computer

- How string players can build skills that take advantage of cinematic music, including recording and arranging

## Benefits When Using Amplification

- Volume control without muscular strain

- Tonal control

- The ability to use a looper pedal

- Access to special effects like wah wah, phase shifter, and delay—on up to 100-plus additional effects through the use of a stomp box

- Bow and left-hand technique can improve because playing on an electric invites a lighter touch on the fingerboard. This, in turn, makes it easier to play faster and supports the production of a more flowing vibrato because the left hand is more relaxed. As that information travels into the bow hand across a gateway between the right and left motor cortices called the corpus callosum, you will benefit from a more relaxed bow hold.

- Better intonation within ensembles, because if you can't hear yourself well during rehearsal and performance, it can be difficult—if not impossible—to play in tune; most likely, greater right- and left-hand pressure will be required to boost volume. Ironically, an increase in pressure can make it more difficult to adjust finger placement. It can also open the doorway to injury. You can also plug into an electronic tuner and have visual proof of flat, in-tune, or sharp pitches. While I don't recommend relying on your eyes to play in tune, this can be a useful training device because of the immediate and honest feedback you'll receive about how you're listening.

### Opportunities for String Orchestra

The incorporation of today's equipment into your tool set for teaching can boost your student's musical skills. Just because you use amplification or an electric instrument in rehearsal, you don't have to include it in the concert.

You can rotate the use of an electric through an acoustic orchestra section to troubleshoot and build better teamwork more easily. During one of my clinics for an American String Teachers Association conference, I used a student orchestra to demonstrate how one electric violin (a five-string will accommodate the violists) and one electric cello could be used to help save time, problem-solve the weakest links in the group, generate heightened ensemble interaction, and provide an opportunity to feature players in an egalitarian manner.

For instance, with the use of a few electrics during orchestra rehearsals, you can skip stand-by-stand searches for the weakest link. Announcing that you're going to pass an electric through each section at the next rehearsal will boost personal practice time. Student musicians, fearing being put on the spot in this manner, will realize they must work harder during their preparatory process or their bad (or nonexistent) practice habits will be revealed to the group. After all, when you're buried in the back of a section, you can fake your way through the music without anyone catching on... except, maybe, your stand partner!

Just rehearse the music and pass the instrument(s) around. Purchase a long guitar cable (see "Cables") and keep the amp near you. This will enable you to control the volume of the amp and quickly determine who is speeding up, stumbling, is having problems with intonation, or playing incorrect notes and/or rhythms.

Ensemble playing always improves when sections learn the focal melodic and rhythmic ideas of the other parts. Using a few electrics, players will easily be able to hear one another's section parts simultaneously. You can also invite a player from each section to pick out and teach seminal lines from their part to the whole group, using call and response on an electric. While this can be achieved on an acoustic instrument, using an electric is easier to hear and makes it more inviting and fun because of the novelty effect. Just a few minutes per rehearsal can make a huge difference and help switch the student's brain hierarchy from visual (looking at the music) to auditory (listening more deeply). If the piece of music incorporates room for improvisation, electrics can be set up at the front of the rehearsal space or stage and soloists can quickly move into place to play at the appropriate time.

You can also work with students to use electric instruments to create a prologue, epilogue, or even lines that accompany a pre-written score. Why not add student-crafted ideas to Tchaikovsky? You may or may not opt to include this in the school concert, but what a lovely way to foster creativity and composition while working on traditional repertoire.

In general, the use of an electric with a looper makes it easier to teach composition and improvisation. Plug the electric into a looping device (a stomp box or app on tablet) to generate layers of ideas. Each new idea that's played has to be done with perfect time and intonation to successfully layer in over pre-recorded ideas. This process also challenges the player to generate new layers while remembering previous ideas, to come up with harmonies and counterpoint, all while maintaining a steady beat. (See "Creative Musicianship: The Looper as a Creative Tool.") I have seen students perform repertoire with greater musicianship after working with the looper. The ability to craft layers of short ideas during practice with the looper requires the same processes a composer might use for longer pieces. This can help build listening and analytic skills which, in turn, will improve the performance of composed pieces.

# AMPLIFICATION AND SPECIAL EFFECTS

There are quite a few options designed to give you control over volume—and, in some cases, tone—depending on whether you wish to boost your acoustic or emulate an electrified type of sound. There are also a number of good arguments for why you should include an electric instrument in your arsenal if you're a string teacher, a pro, or an amateur. Even if you don't picture yourself venturing in this direction, learning the basics about amplification will help prepare you for every eventuality.

## How to Amplify Bowed Strings

- Play into a standing microphone or use a small clip-on mic.

- Attach a pickup to the bridge or buy a bridge that has a transducer already embedded in its wood and replace your acoustic bridge with the transducer bridge.

- Purchase a solid-body electric that has no acoustic sound and must be plugged into an amp to be heard.

## The Mic

A good quality microphone will provide the truest representation of your instrument's tone. There are two options available:

1) You can purchase a microphone that attaches to a stand. The stand should be a boom stand so that you can position the microphone with adequate distance from its pole, otherwise your bow will mostly likely hit the pole unless you lean over while playing. This solution will reduce mobility, which is why I recommend the second option.

Mics can pick up ambient sound, so if you plan to play with a large ensemble and will be standing next to percussion or horns, this may not be the best option. You will also need to boost your volume in large ensembles, which can sometimes lead to feedback or distortion.

2) You can use a clip-on mic that's been designed specifically to accommodate bowed strings, like the Bartlett mic that attaches under the tailpiece using a light block of foam. If the mic clips onto the bridge, it will obviously be amplifying a muffled sound. Therefore, a mic that can clip onto or tuck underneath the tailpiece is a better option.

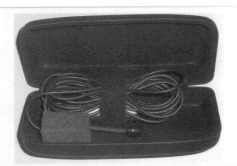

## Pickups

Pickups that attach to the bridge are also available for amplification. Remember, anything that touches the bridge will modify your instrument's sound—usually not for the better—though a preamp or good amp can help compensate for any loss of tone.

Some pickups have less capability to deal with high-volume situations than others, so make sure you read reviews before purchase. Even the best pickup, professionally installed and supported by a great preamp, may not enable you to hear yourself when jamming with 20 conga drum players.

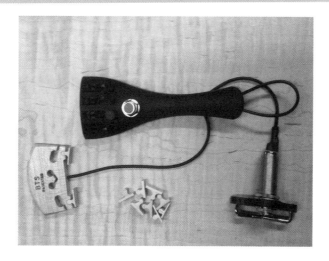

### Transducer Bridge

A transducer bridge generally boosts the outgoing signal significantly more than a pickup because the electronics are built into it. This type of bridge has a wire coming out of it that attaches into a fixture clamped onto the purfling of your instrument. There's a guitar jack installed into that fixture so you can plug one end of a guitar cable into the fixture and the other into your preamp or amp. Sometimes the use of a transducer bridge can alter the tone of your acoustic instrument—for the better or for the worse, depending on the maker. It's recommended that you have this type of bridge installed on a second instrument. Factor in the cost of having the bridge shaped by a luthier to fit your instrument.

Some companies, like L.R. Baggs and the Barbera Transducer System, make sure the construction of the bridge compensates for the electronics built into it. You can also use a preamp to provide additional tonal control.

### Solid-Body

The solid-body violin, viola, or cello has little or no sound when played acoustically. It has to be plugged into an amp to be heard. There is no danger of feedback (an unpleasant high-pitched squawk) when you boost the volume, and most solid-body instruments will provide you with all the volume you need. You can also choose between fairly tame-looking instruments or really flashy designs that distinguish you when you step onstage.

Some solid-body instruments require batteries. Think ahead and picture the situations this instrument will be used in. Ask yourself if you'll be able to carry back-up batteries or purchase them wherever you plan to use the instrument, particularly if a nine-volt battery is called for. Factor in the weight batteries can add to an instrument and make sure you're okay with supporting that weight across the hours of practice, performance, and travel.

### Solid-Body with MIDI

You can attach any kind of electric instrument to certain music editing and recording software programs via a guitar cable by purchasing that company's interface. This usually consists of a small box with a guitar cable input and USB output. However, if you desire the ability to use a computer program that transcribes what you play, or a system that will add control over the sounds your instrument emits (like making your instrument sound like a flute or even like percussion), then you will need an instrument that has MIDI (Musical Instrument Digital Interface) capability. This means the electronics configured for that instrument must be capable of translating sound through certain synthesizer brands. Use your browser to search for a list of interfaces by typing in "MIDI violin, viola, or cello" or "MIDI bowed strings" to find specific companies and the equipment you'll need.

### The Preamp

The preamp is a small box you can use as an intermediary between your pickup and amp or house system. It provides tonal control, as well as the capability to boost the volume. It also supplies the player with close-at-hand control over the equalization (treble, mid-range, and bass ratios). Note that some pickup systems come with their own companion preamp.

## The Amp

No pickup or solid-body is effective without an amp. Purchasing decisions should be based on budget, volume requirements, the tone, and transportation concerns since some models are heavy. Always have extra guitar cables on hand. To play in tune, you obviously will need to hear yourself adequately. If you're playing on a solid-body, be prepared to place the amp on a chair or stand directly behind where you plan to sit or stand; if using a mic, place the amp slightly off-angle to avoid feedback. You can also place it in front of you, but be sure to tilt the amp toward your head. Otherwise the sound will project across the floor, which might be useful to your feet, but not your ears.

## Electronic Effects

You can purchase a single electronic effect in a stomp box, or plug your instrument into one single unit that offers close to 100 options. Each effect will alter your instrument's sound. Here are a few of the more popular effects:

- Digital delay creates an echo

- Phase shifter fattens the sound and gives it a spatial quality

- Octaver adds a second note an octave below, though some boxes provide a harmonizer that can be tuned to other intervals

- Distortion provides an electric guitar rock-esque quality

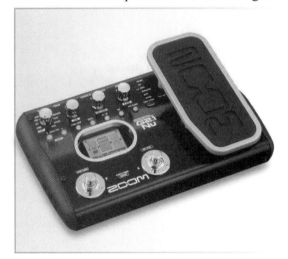

Or you can opt for a stomp box like the one made by the company Zoom. It is relatively inexpensive and offers a wide range of effects to choose from. Some units also include a looper that's capable of recording and layering only four- to six-beat phrases, whereas a stomp box dedicated to looping might record up to four hours of music.

There are a few companies that make multi-style stomp boxes, so how do you decide which one to buy? Read the reviews and look for comments like, "I could read the LCD screen easily when I looked down at the floor." Or, "It only took me a few minutes to figure out how to use it." I like Zoom because it allows me to change the tonal settings on each effect to accommodate my taste; it also allows me to save the effects I use the most often into the bank of my choice so I can move gracefully through my favorites while playing.

## Cables

Make sure you have at least one long and two shorter guitar cables. These are also known as quarter-inch cables and I always travel with extras just in case. You will need the guitar cable to connect your solid-body or transducer bridge into a preamp, stomp box, and/or amplifier. I always have at least one elbow-shaped cable on hand; that way, when I plug that side of the cable into my instrument, I don't end up with a straight plug that either sticks into me or can catch on anything or anyone around me.

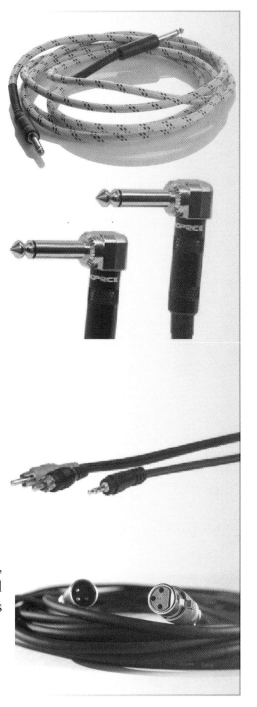

My favorite elbow-shaped cable has a kill switch. This is a button that enables me to interrupt the signal from my instrument to my amp in case I want to tune or avoid a loud "pop" if I need to unplug the cable. There are a few other cables you need to know about that are handy to have available.

The stereo plug (also called an audio cable or RCA plug) to mini-plug is a must-have if:

- You want to run an accompaniment from iTunes, or whatever music program you use, from your Smartphone or tablet into a mixer

- You want to use apps in your Smartphone or tablet and listen to what you're played or have recorded through your amplifier or home sound system.

The XLR cable will be needed only if you use a microphone. It's also handy to have a converter on hand: XLR to guitar plug. This is in case you want to plug your mic into a stomp box or preamp, or if your amp doesn't have an XLR input, since some amps and all stomp boxes only come with quarter-inch jacks. Here is what this type of jack looks like:

## Apps for Tablet or Smartphone

It's also possible to interface a solid-body instrument with your tablet or smartphone. There are hundreds of apps to choose from that will provide you with special effects, eight-track recording studios, and looping capability.

To run sounds from your instrument through a tablet or smartphone, you will need an interface that allows you to plug your instrument in via a guitar cable. The interface comes with its own connector that fits your Smartphone or tablet.

You will also require the free app, Audiobus, which you can download from the app store. This app acts like a traffic cop; it alerts your tablet or phone to receive audio from your instrument and directs incoming notes through whichever music app you've chosen to work with.

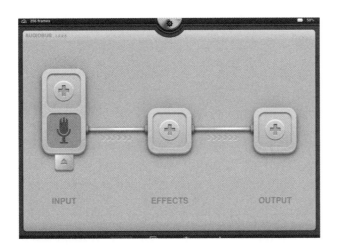

Always read reviews before choosing apps to download. Look for words like "intuitive," "easy to learn," and "free." Some apps cost nothing to download and use, but then offer in-app purchases. This means that if you want to add more capability to the app, you will have to pay. Usually these costs are minimal, though.

# HOW DO I CHOOSE WHAT TO BUY?

Thankfully, new equipment becomes available every year and the choices keep improving. In general, though, you need to factor in at least four considerations before choosing the best option for yourself or your string program:

- Budget

- Volume

- Timbre

- Comfort

## Budget

Once you establish what you can afford to pay, make sure you factor in the cost of an amp, a preamp (discussed earlier), some quarter-inch guitar cables to connect your instrument to the amp, special effects, a looper, and/or preamp. A couple of long cables and a few shorter ones should set you up to get started. (See "Cables.") You might want to have a few spare cables on hand in case you lose one or a cable goes bad. You should also plan for extra batteries for any of those extra boxes between your instrument and the amp, in case you're in a situation where you aren't able to run out to a store.

## Volume

Before choosing an appropriate system, assess the environments you will be rehearsing/performing in—such as band size, instrumentation, and solo over a group accompaniment versus integral to the band or ensemble. As discussed earlier, there are limits to how much volume one can achieve from a pickup mounted on the instrument. There's a trade-off when you choose a solid-body: It can project a lot of volume, but tends to eliminate some, if not all, of the acoustic tonal quality. The instrument can literally sound electric, though nowadays we're able to work miracles with our amplification equipment to warm up the tone.

## Timbre

Mics and transducer bridges generally offer a warmer sound than solid-body, but so much of this is influenced by the preamp and amp that it's important to try it all out at a local music store or a friend or colleague's home before investing in a full system.

Controlling one's tone isn't that different on an electric than an acoustic. We finesse our sound post setting, the carving of the bridge, the type of strings we use, and the bow to elicit the best possible sound. Same process, different equipment, when it comes to an electric instrument.

When I presented my "Going Electric" clinic at the International Association for Jazz Educators conference, I invited eight of my colleagues to bring their electric instruments. We had a lineup of the absolute best players—including Darol Anger, Tracy Silverman, and Christian Howes—on the best possible array of equipment. I invited each player to play through the same amp, and then again through a second amp. Each instrument sounded entirely different through each of the two amps. This test proved that if you choose an instrument based on its look rather than its tone, you will be able to manipulate its sound with a mixer, preamp, or amp.

## Comfort

When choosing a solid-body violin or viola, make sure the instrument isn't too heavy or uncomfortable to play before you purchase it. Some designs offer a great deal of flexibility as to the type of shoulder rest and chin rest you can use, while others deliver scant choices.

If you're a cellist, make sure you have options for placement as well. How long is the endpin? Does the instrument strap on? If so, is the strap adjustable enough to suit your frame? Do you have the physical strength required to support its weight?

Also, if the manufacturer supplies a case, consider the type of case the instrument comes in. For instance, if you've spent every penny you have and then realize the case has too short a shoulder strap to carry the instrument comfortably, is too flimsy or heavy, you're looking at another expenditure for a case that meets your needs.

It's important to provide yourself with an opportunity to play for at least a half hour on the instrument you're interested in purchasing, to make sure it's a good partner for your body-type and needs.

## A Few Other Considerations

### Fine Tuners

Besides the fact that well-fitted pegs are not always a luxury found on instruments in a $2,500 (and under) range, fine tuners are a must when it comes to playing on an amplified instrument. The use of fine tuners for each of the four strings is an excellent way to make fast, subtle adjustments while amplified.

### Strings

I particularly recommend D'Addario's Helicore and Zyex strings. For alternative styles, these strings provide a smoother surface for slide technique and give softer resistance to the left-hand fingers. They break in quickly and sound great.

### Instructional Materials

Sometimes, the manual that comes with equipment isn't written clearly. If you're like me, you learn more quickly from seeing demonstrations than reading a manual, anyway. Use YouTube instructional videos to master any hardware or software you choose to purchase.

# HOW TO CREATE YOUR OWN BACKING TRACKS

The melody for a tune constitutes only half of the total sound each style offers. That's because the style-specific instruments and the arrangement within which the melody is framed account for a large percentage of the total effect. Band students practice and perform with a rhythm section from day one, but string players are not provided with this opportunity. This makes it harder for us to capture any style outside our personal training.

To develop the proper articulation and genre-appropriate groove for styles other than that of Western Europe, it's important to practice with the appropriate accompaniment. Since this is not possible to do live—unless you've formed an ensemble or band with the correct instrumentation—you can improve playing capabilities by generating and practicing with backing tracks.

There are two methods you can use to create style-specific backing tracks:

1) Hire musicians and record the backing tracks you need for future use. Since hiring musicians is not a possibility for most of us, let's take a closer look at our other option.

2) Use a software program like Band in a Box and purchase extra style packs appropriate to your chosen genre.

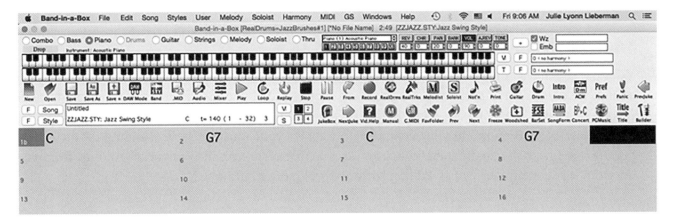

The most basic level of this software program by PG Music includes an enormous number of styles and options in the software package, and additional style packs can be purchased. This program is as easy as typing in a few chords, choosing a style, and hitting play. You can change the length of the accompaniment, key, or tempo in just a few seconds. The software package includes MIDI as well as real instruments.

# RECORDING AND ARRANGING

There are a number of good reasons to have equipment or software available with which you can record yourself.

- You can improve your musicianship quickly by recording and then listening back to the pieces you're currently working on.

- You can use tracks you record to get work, audition for a school or program, or to post to YouTube to build a following.

- Whether you're a director who wants to raise money for your string program or you're an artist who wants to sell your music, you can record a piece of music and upload it into an account you open on CD Baby Now. This company will post your recording to iTunes and you can also sell the track through your personal page on CD Baby Now.

- You will be able to generate your own ringtones and give them as a personalized gift to friends and family by using any one of a number of smartphone or tablet apps now available for just such a purpose.

- You can record from the privacy of your own home or from your classroom without paying to rent a studio with an engineer. This will enable you to re-record your track(s) as many times as you wish until you are thoroughly satisfied with the outcome.

- You will be able to generate your own backing tracks and your own creative output.

## An Overview of the Equipment You'll Need

You can use either computer software, an app on your tablet, or a digital recorder. Ultimately, whatever you use will have to offer the capacity to link to your computer for upload. Though you may only be interested in burning your recording directly to CD, you will also be able to modify tonal settings and edit the recording using music software like Cubase, ProTools, or Logic. There are light versions of these programs that keep the prices low.

## Digital Recorder

With the advent of computers, the recording industry now offers a number of solutions for recording straight into your computer, using the programs mentioned above. But if you need to use a portable recorder, it's best to purchase something like the Zoom digital recorder. It is packaged with the appropriate cord to plug into your computer to transfer your music files. Depending on the device, your music files will usually transfer in as aif or wav files. You can then import those files from your desktop or storage folder into an editing software program or burn to CD.

# CINEMATIC MUSIC FOR STRINGS

As mentioned in the unit "Practice Techniques," we tend to define ear training through a traditional lens as an aural skill based on identifying pitch, intervals, melody, chords, rhythms, and other basic elements of music. The field of music for cinema, video games, and television provides new focal points to help develop listening skills in new directions. Participation in this field can also potentially challenge you to combine creativity, composition, and improvisation with arranging and recording skills.

Video game music sales outperform sales for Hollywood movie music. Both industries—including music for television shows and commercials—rely on industry-tailored compositions. This music has an important task: to convey moods, pre-shadow storyline changes, and offer signature themes that represent specific characters or scenes. String players and students are exposed to the music of this industry every single day, but there are few, if any, dedicated support materials that provide tangible tools to enter the field, or at least to take advantage of the learning possibilities. Jobs for professional string players tap into good sight-reading and solid playing skills learned from classical training; unfortunately, composition, arranging, and recording are not included as "must haves" in a string player's educational process.

There are four opportunities available when teaching or studying cinematic music:

1) You can learn to identify the difference between music designed to accompany visual stories versus concert music and integrate that knowledge into your playing skills.

2) You can add texture to your playing by venturing outside of melody and harmony through the generation of textural effects inspired by emotions and visual topography.

3) You can write a story and compose (or improvise) music to accompany the story.

4) You can develop your arranging skills by learning to choose and couple soundtrack loops with a pre-written melody or orchestra arrangement.

## Cinematic Music Exercises

### Textural Music

Make sure you understand the difference between playing a melody, a rhythmic accompaniment, harmony, or a texture. To widen your vocabulary of textures, first start with classical techniques like tremolo (a fast, light bow-stroke played at the tip using short bows) or pizzicato. Then experiment with generating textures on your instrument by searching for your own sounds.

### Emotional Colors

Create a list of adjectives, emotions, and colors.

Borrow a short melodic line from a tune, piece of music, or score of your choice. Choose an adjective, emotion, or color from your list and challenge yourself (or your students) to play an interpretation of the melodic line through that filter. This is subtle. How do you convey the same melody through the lens of anger, the color blue, the adjective "happy" versus "sad," a timid bird, a train, or to express danger?

Experiment with rhythmic and tempo adjustments, volume, and bowings as needed. It can help to focus on one of your senses: touch, smell, taste. What sounds might convey the feeling of touching a cactus? Of tasting an orange? Of smelling smoke from a fire?

**Identify the difference between music designed to accompany visual stories versus concert music:**

Sometimes the line is quite thin between concert and cinematic music, so you might want to compare examples. Find a piece of recorded classical music by a famous composer, a second classical piece that's been used at least once for film (refer to iTunes, *Classical Music Used for Cinema: Top 200 Movie Classics*), and then listen to and cross-compare with a piece of music from a movie that's currently trending. Try to identify the similarities and the differences.

For instance, work with the standing question, "How is *incidental music* different?" Yes, it's designed to weave a specific atmosphere, but how does it accomplish that?

You can use this as an opportunity to ask questions, like "How does this music make me feel?" or "What type of scene do I think is taking place in the movie when I hear this music?"

Often, scenes from movies or television shows are available on YouTube and you can isolate the music to study it by using free online software that extracts music from videos for download.

Teachers, invite your students to bring in music from video games or their favorite TV show or movie. Challenge them to identify the difference between a theme song and incidental music, or ask your students to play a favorite theme song by ear by picking out the notes on violin, viola, or cello.

## Cinematic Music Tracks

When a composer designs cinematic music, he or she may work with a number of programs:

- Notation software, like Finale or Sibelius

- Recording and arranging software, like ProTools, Logic, or Cubase (There are also inexpensive apps available for tablet, but with far less capability.)

- Loops

The term "loop" in this context refers to a commercially available pre-recorded soundtrack. It can be as short as one single hit on a bass drum, a 15-second percussion track, a walking bass line, or any number of instrumental sounds.

Loops are sold by online companies and, short of hiring a full orchestra and recording engineers, help you create moods and effects. For instance, you can purchase the sound of a clock ticking, the wind blowing, thunder, the sound of a horse's hooves galloping, various types of drums from around the world, and many more. The possibilities are so numerous it would be impossible to list them all here. Garage Band, which comes free in most computers and is packaged with a limited number of loops, is a simplified software program that can help you get started if you wish to learn about how to generate your own backing tracks or recordings.

When I composed my *Bollywood Strings* string orchestra score, I exported the composition from Finale as an audio file to use as a template. Then I imported that file into Cubase and designed a backing track for rehearsal and performance. I purchased authentic Indian instrument loops and numerous sound effects from Internet-based companies to work with after listening through hundreds of samples. Then, I configured Cubase so that each loop was automatically adjusted to the metronomic value and key to match the tempo and key for the *Bollywood Strings* score.

Ultimately, the arrangement used 45 tracks in Cubase to layer these effects, dovetailing some while weaving others from start to finish. The end result was a Bollywood-style backup track that interlocks with the written score.

# INDEX

**JULIE LYONN LIEBERMAN** has helped develop the alternative string field as a performer, educator, author, composer, radio and concert producer, and recording artist. She is the Artistic Director for the summer program, *Strings Without Boundaries*. Ms. Lieberman is also an NS Design Performance Artist and a D'Addario Premiere Clinician.

Lieberman co-authored American String Teachers Association's national curriculum book, "Standards, Goals, and Learning Sequences for Essential Skills and Knowledge in K-12 String Programs," and is the author of seven music books and six educational DVDs, as well as 20+ string orchestra scores in American and world styles (Kendor Music, Alfred Music and Carl Fischer).

She is the recipient of the 2014 ASTA Kudos Award, over two-dozen ASCAP Plus Awards, and three American String Teachers Association's National Citation for Leadership & Merit awards. She has written and produced two National Public Radio Series: *The Talking Violin*, hosted by Dr. Billy Taylor, and *Jazz Profiles: Jazz Violin* hosted by Nancy Wilson.

Ms. Lieberman has taught creative musicianship and world string styles in school residencies and teacher trainings across the United States and beyond as well as through organizations and institutions like American String Teachers Association, European String Teachers Association, National Orchestra Festival, National Association for Music Education, International Association of Jazz Educators, The Midwest Clinic, The Starling-Delay Symposium, Suzuki Institute, National String Workshop, International String Workshop, Django in June, The Juilliard MAP Program, National Young Audiences, the Carnegie Hall LinkUp Program, and The Academy (produced by Carnegie/Weill Hall/Juilliard).

# The Violin Play-Along Series

## Play your favorite songs quickly and easily!

Just follow the music, listen to the CD or online audio to hear how the violin should sound, and then play along using the separate backing tracks. The audio files are enhanced so you can adjust the recordings to any tempo without changing pitch!

**1. Bluegrass**
00842152 Book/CD Pack .........$14.99

**2. Popular Songs**
00842153 Book/CD Pack .........$14.99

**3. Classical**
00842154 Book/CD Pack .........$14.99

**4. Celtic**
00842155 Book/CD Pack .........$14.99

**5. Christmas Carols**
00842156 Book/Online Audio ..$14.99

**6. Holiday Hits**
00842157 Book/CD Pack .........$14.99

**7. Jazz**
00842196 Book/CD Pack .........$14.99

**8. Country Classics**
00842230 Book/CD Pack .........$12.99

**9. Country Hits**
00842231 Book/CD Pack .........$14.99

**10. Bluegrass Favorites**
00842232 Book/CD Pack .........$14.99

**11. Bluegrass Classics**
00842233 Book/CD Pack .........$14.99

**12. Wedding Classics**
00842324 Book/CD Pack .........$14.99

**13. Wedding Favorites**
00842325 Book/CD Pack .........$14.99

**14. Blues Classics**
00842427 Book/CD Pack .........$14.99

**15. Stephane Grappelli**
00842428 Book/CD Pack .........$14.99

**16. Folk Songs**
00842429 Book/CD Pack ..........$14.99

**17. Christmas Favorites**
00842478 Book/CD Pack .........$14.99

**18. Fiddle Hymns**
00842499 Book/CD Pack ..........$14.99

**19. Lennon & McCartney**
00842564 Book/CD Pack ..........$14.99

**20. Irish Tunes**
00842565 Book/CD Pack ..........$14.99

**21. Andrew Lloyd Webber**
00842566 Book/CD Pack ..........$14.99

**22. Broadway Hits**
00842567 Book/CD Pack ..........$14.99

**23. Pirates of the Caribbean**
00842625 Book/CD Pack ..........$14.99

**24. Rock Classics**
00842640 Book/CD Pack ..........$14.99

**25. Classical Masterpieces**
00842642 Book/CD Pack ..........$14.99

**26. Elementary Classics**
00842643 Book/CD Pack ..........$14.99

**27. Classical Favorites**
00842646 Book/CD Pack ..........$14.99

**28. Classical Treasures**
00842647 Book/CD Pack ..........$14.99

**29. Disney Favorites**
00842648 Book/CD Pack ..........$14.99

**30. Disney Hits**
00842649 Book/CD Pack ..........$14.99

**31. Movie Themes**
00842706 Book/CD Pack ..........$14.99

**32. Favorite Christmas Songs**
00102110 Book/CD Pack ..........$14.99

**33. Hoedown**
00102161 Book/CD Pack ..........$14.99

**34. Barn Dance**
00102568 Book/CD Pack ..........$14.99

**35. Lindsey Stirling**
00109715 Book/CD Pack ..........$19.99

**36. Hot Jazz**
00110373 Book/CD Pack ..........$14.99

**37. Taylor Swift**
00116361 Book/CD Pack ..........$14.99

**38. John Williams**
00116367 Book/CD Pack ..........$14.99

**39. Italian Songs**
00116368 Book/CD Pack ..........$14.99

**41. Johann Strauss**
00121041 Book/CD Pack ..........$14.99

**42. Light Classics**
00121935 Book/Online Audio ...$14.99

**43. Light Orchestra Pop**
00122126 Book/Online Audio ...$14.99

**44. French Songs**
00122123 Book/Online Audio ...$14.99

**45. Lindsey Stirling Hits**
00123128 Book/Online Audio ...$19.99

**46. Piazzolla Tangos**
48022997 Book/Online Audio ...$16.99

**47. Light Masterworks**
00124149 Book/Online Audio ...$14.99

**48. Frozen**
00126478 Book/Online Audio ...$14.99

**49. Pop/Rock**
00130216 Book/Online Audio ...$14.99

**50. Songs for Beginners**
00131417 Book/Online Audio ...$14.99

**51. Chart Hits for Beginners**
00131418 Book/Online Audio ...$14.99

**53. Rockin' Classics**
00148768 Book/Online Audio ...$14.99

**54. Scottish Folksongs**
00148779 Book/Online Audio ...$14.99

**55. Wicked**
00148780 Book/Online Audio ...$14.99

**56. The Sound of Music**
00148782 Book/Online Audio ...$14.99

**58. The Piano Guys – Wonders**
00151837 Book/Online Audio ...$19.99

Disney characters and artwork © Disney Enterprises, Inc.

Prices, contents, and availability subject to change without notice.

7777 W. Bluemound Rd. P.O. Box 13819 Milwaukee, WI 53213

**www.halleonard.com**

0915

# 101 SONGS

## YOUR FAVORITE SONGS ARE ARRANGED JUST FOR SOLO INSTRUMENTALISTS WITH THIS GREAT SERIES.

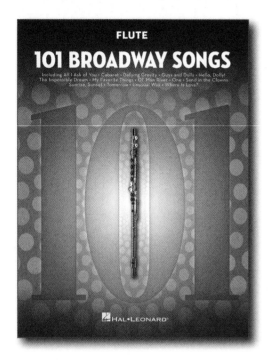

**FLUTE**
**101 BROADWAY SONGS**

**VIOLIN**
**101 CLASSICAL THEMES**

**TRUMPET**
**101 JAZZ SONGS**

### 101 BROADWAY SONGS

Any Dream Will Do • Cabaret • Defying Gravity • Do You Hear the People Sing? • Edelweiss • Getting to Know You • Guys and Dolls • Hello, Dolly! • I Dreamed a Dream • If I Were a Bell • Luck Be a Lady • Mame • The Music of the Night • Ol' Man River • People Will Say We're in Love • Seasons of Love • Send in the Clowns • The Surrey with the Fringe on Top • Think of Me • Tomorrow • What I Did for Love • You'll Never Walk Alone • and many more.

| | | |
|---|---|---|
| 00154199 | Flute | $14.99 |
| 00154200 | Clarinet | $14.99 |
| 00154201 | Alto Sax | $14.99 |
| 00154202 | Tenor Sax | $14.99 |
| 00154203 | Trumpet | $14.99 |
| 00154204 | Horn | $14.99 |
| 00154205 | Trombone | $14.99 |
| 00154206 | Violin | $14.99 |
| 00154207 | Viola | $14.99 |
| 00154208 | Cello | $14.99 |

### 101 CLASSICAL THEMES

Ave Maria • Bist du bei mir (You Are with Me) • Canon in D • Clair de Lune • Dance of the Sugar Plum Fairy • 1812 Overture • Eine Kleine Nachtmusik ("Serenade"), First Movement Excerpt • The Flight of the Bumble Bee • Funeral March of a Marionette • Fur Elise • Gymnopedie No. 1 • Jesu, Joy of Man's Desiring • Lullaby • Minuet in G • Ode to Joy • Piano Sonata in C • Pie Jesu • Rondeau • Theme from Swan Lake • Wedding March • William Tell Overture • and many more.

| | | |
|---|---|---|
| 00155315 | Flute | $14.99 |
| 00155317 | Clarinet | $14.99 |
| 00155318 | Alto Sax | $14.99 |
| 00155319 | Tenor Sax | $14.99 |
| 00155320 | Trumpet | $14.99 |
| 00155321 | Horn | $14.99 |
| 00155322 | Trombone | $14.99 |
| 00155323 | Violin | $14.99 |
| 00155324 | Viola | $14.99 |
| 00155325 | Cello | $14.99 |

### 101 JAZZ SONGS

All of Me • Autumn Leaves • Bewitched • Blue Skies • Body and Soul • Cheek to Cheek • Come Rain or Come Shine • Don't Get Around Much Anymore • A Fine Romance • Here's to Life • I Could Write a Book • It Could Happen to You • The Lady Is a Tramp • Like Someone in Love • Lullaby of Birdland • The Nearness of You • On Green Dolphin Street • Satin Doll • Stella by Starlight • Tangerine • Unforgettable • The Way You Look Tonight • Yesterdays • and many more.

| | | |
|---|---|---|
| 00146363 | Flute | $14.99 |
| 00146364 | Clarinet | $14.99 |
| 00146366 | Alto Sax | $14.99 |
| 00146367 | Tenor Sax | $14.99 |
| 00146368 | Trumpet | $14.99 |
| 00146369 | Horn | $14.99 |
| 00146370 | Trombone | $14.99 |
| 00146371 | Violin | $14.99 |
| 00146372 | Viola | $14.99 |
| 00146373 | Cello | $14.99 |

**HAL•LEONARD® CORPORATION**
7777 W. BLUEMOUND RD. P.O. BOX 13819 MILWAUKEE, WI 53213

*Prices, contents and availability subject to change without notice.*

www.halleonard.com